Daily Discoveries

for February

Thematic Learning Activities for

EVERY DAY

Written by Elizabeth Cole Midg

Illustrated by Jennette Guymon-Kin

Teaching & Learning Company

1204 Buchanan St., P.O. Box 10

Carthage, IL 62321-0010

This book belongs to

_____

Several of the activities in this book involve preparing, tasting and sharing food items. We urge you to be aware of any food allergies or restrictions your students may have and to supervise these activities diligently. All food-related suggestions are identified with this allergy-alert symbol: ⚠

Please note: small food items (candies, raisins, cereal, etc.) can also pose a choking hazard.

Cover art by Jennette Guymon-King

Copyright © 2005, Teaching & Learning Company

ISBN No. 1-57310-467-1

Printing No. 987654321

Teaching & Learning Company
1204 Buchanan St., P.O. Box 10
Carthage, IL 62321-0010

At the time of publication every effort was made to insure the accuracy of the information included in this book. However, we cannot guarantee that agencies and organizations mentioned will continue to operate or maintain these current locations.

Table of Contents

Dear Teacher or Parent,

Due to the stimulus of a high-tech world, parents and teachers are often faced with the challenge of how to capture the attention of a child and create an atmosphere of meaningful learning opportunities. Often we search for new ways to meet this challenge and help young people transfer their knowledge, skills and experiences from one area to another. Subjects taught in isolation can leave a feeling of fragmentation. More and more educators are looking for ways to be able to integrate curriculum so that their students can fully understand how things relate to each other.

The Daily Discoveries series has been developed to that end. The premise behind this series has been, in part, the author's educational philosophy: anything can be taught and absorbed by others in a meaningful way, depending upon its presentation.

In this series, each day has been researched around the history of a specific individual or event and has been developed into a celebration or theme with integrated curriculum areas. In this approach to learning students draw from their own experience and understanding of things, to a level of processing new information and skills.

The Daily Discoveries series is an almanac-of-sorts, 12 books (one for each month) that present a thematically based curriculum for grades K-6. The series contains hundreds and hundreds of resources and ideas that can be a natural springboard to learning. These ideas have been used in the classroom and at home, and are fun as well as educationally sound. The activities have been endorsed by professors, teachers, parents and, best of all, by children.

The Daily Discoveries series can be used in the following ways for school or home:
- to develop new skills and reinforce previous learning
- to create a sense of fun and celebration every day
- as tutoring resources
- as enrichment activities that can be used as time allows
- for family fun activities

Sincerely,

Elizabeth

Elizabeth Cole Midgley

Robinson Crusoe Day

February 1

Setting the Stage
- Display island "souvenirs" (seashells, fish, coconuts, palm trees, etc.) around a copy of the book *Robinson Crusoe* by Daniel Defoe.

Historical Background
In September 1704, a Scottish sailor named Alexander Selkirk was put ashore on an uninhabited island at his own request after an argument with his captain. He was rescued on February 1, 1709. His adventures were the basis for the legendary Robinson Crusoe.

Literary Exploration
The New Robinson Crusoe by Joachim Heinrich Campe
Robinson Crusoe by Daniel Defoe
Robinson Crusoe: Retold for Today's Children by Anne deGraf
Selkirk's Island by Diana Souhami
Swiss Family Robinson by Johann Wyss

Language Experience
• Challenge students to come up with as many adjectives as they can to describe what it would be like to live on a deserted island.

Writing Experience

• Have students write postcards home from Robinson Crusoe's perspective.

• Let students imagine they are all alone on an island. Have them write journal entries to describe how they got there and what happens to them.

Science/Health Experience

• Challenge students to consider Robinson Crusoe's nutritional needs. What did he find to eat? What kinds of foods were good for him? What did he need that he did not have to stay healthy?

Social Studies Experience

• Have students research life in the early 1700s in Great Britain. What would life as a sailor be like? What things would Robinson Crusoe not have missed that we would miss today? (electricity, running water, etc.)

Music/Dramatic Experience
• Let students pretend they meet another person after being alone on an island for years. How would they act? Let partners act out their feelings.

Physical/Sensory Experience
• What exercise did Robinson Crusoe do to stay fit? Challenge students to create some exercises that would help keep them in shape if they were marooned on a deserted island.

Arts/Crafts Experience

• Let students work together to turn a corner of your classroom into an island. Provide some sand and shells. Construct palm trees by wrapping cardboard tubes with brown crepe paper, then cutting big leaves from green paper and taping them to the trunks. Others may draw a long ocean, sunset scene on mural paper. Let them go to the island corner to read when they finish their work early.

Extension Activities

• Challenge students to bring two items from home that they feel would be absolutely invaluable if they were stranded on a deserted island. The items must be small enough to fit in a suitcase. Have students explain why their items would be indispensable.

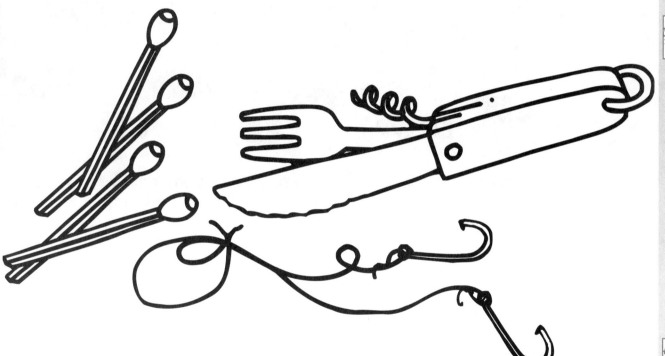

Values Education Experience

• Ask students to share why living alone on an island for an extended time would be a difficult adventure. Discuss feelings such as loneliness and fear. Talk about the advantage of having other people around to talk with, do things with and enjoy. But it's also important to be somewhat self-reliant, able to be by ourselves sometimes.

Groundhog
Day

Groundhog
Day

Groundhog
Day

Groundhog Day

February 2

Setting the Stage

- Display student pictures or silhouettes (see page 14) with the caption: "Without a SHADOW of a doubt, you're fantastic!"

- Put "shadow footprints" (made out of black construction paper) on the floor leading into the classroom or walking up a wall.

- Construct a semantic map or web with facts students already know about groundhogs or shadows. Then ask them to list what they would like to learn about today.

Historical Background

In German folklore a groundhog comes out of hibernation on this day every year. If the groundhog sees its shadow (because the sun is shining), it will return to its burrow for another six weeks of winter. If it does not see its shadow, there will be an early spring. Pennsylvania Germans celebrated the first Groundhog Day in 1887 in a town called Punxsutawney. Every year residents watch for Punxsutawney Phil, the groundhog they claim has never been wrong in over a hundred years!

Yahoo!
Six more weeks
of winter!

8

Literary Exploration

Bear Shadow by Frank Asch
Clare and Her Shadow by William Michaels
Forecast by Malcolm Hall
Groundhog Day: Story by Sharon Shebar
Groundhog's Day at the Doctor by Judy Delton
Henry in Shadowland by Laszlo Varvasovszky
It's Groundhog Day! by Steven Kroll
Light and Shadow by Myra Cohn Livingston
Mr. Wink and His Shadow, Ned by Dick Gackenbach
Nothing Sticks Like a Shadow by Ann Tompert
Shadow by Marcia Brown
Shadow by Blaise Cendrars
The Shadow Book by Beatrice Schenk De Regniers
Shadow Chaser by Stephen Cosgrove
The Shadow of Matilda Hunt by Deborah Zemke
Shadow Play by Paul Fleischman
The Shadow Shop by Kristin Pedersen
"Shadows" an excerpt from *I Wonder Why Soap Makes Bubbles and
    Other Questions About Science* by Barbara Taylor
Shadows and Reflections by Tana Hoban
Shadowville by Michael Bartalos
The Story of Punxsutawney Phil: The Fearless Forecaster by Julia
    Spencer Moutran
You'll Never Guess! by Fiona Dunbar

Language Experience

• Challenge students to say the tongue twister, "How much wood
  could a woodchuck chuck if a woodchuck could chuck wood?"

• Have students brainstorm other animal compound words besides
  groundhog (such as *woodchuck* or *starfish*).

Groundhog
Day

Groundhog
Day

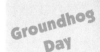

Groundhog
Day

Writing Experience

• Would your students like to sleep for a whole winter? What would they miss? What would they dream about? Let them write their ideas. See reproducible on page 15.

Math Experience

• Let students have fun with math "burrows." Give challenging math problems orally and let them come out from their "burrows" (under their desks) when they know the answers. Competing on teams will add a little excitement!

• Have students measure one another's shadows in the morning, then again in the afternoon and note the differences.

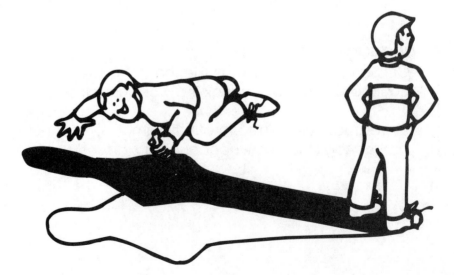

Science/Health Experience

- Begin weather tracking to see if what the Groundhog predicts comes true. Students can record their daily findings in a log-shaped weather "log."

- Begin a unit of study on shadows and light.

- Study groundhogs. Learn how and where they live.

- Students will enjoy making a homemade sun-dial by putting a straight stick into the ground, then drawing a circle around it. Throughout the day they can look at the shadow of the stick to see time passing.

- Leave two pieces of construction paper, one black and one white, outside in the sun. Allow some time to pass, then let students place a hand on each paper to feel the difference between them. The black paper will feel warmer because the sun's rays are absorbed by the darker color more easily.

Social Studies Experience

- Research areas of the world where groundhogs are found, then have students find these areas on a map.

Music/Dramatic Experience

- Check out the song, "Me and My Shadow," to play for the class.

Groundhog Day

Groundhog Day

Groundhog Day

Physical/Sensory Experience

• Have a "shadow theatre!" Students love making shadow puppets on the wall! Simply hang a projector screen or white butcher paper on a wall, turn on a filmstrip projector or bright flashlight and let students use their fingers and imagination to provide the rest!

• Play Groundhog Tag. One person is the groundhog, curled up in a ball. Other students chant to the groundhog, asking if he will wake up today. When the groundhog answers that he will, he chases students, tagging as many as he can. The others run to their burrows to hide (curling up). Anyone who is caught becomes a groundhog, too.

• Early in the morning, take students outside. Let each choose a partner. Let them pick designated areas on the sidewalk to trace one another's shadows in colored chalk. Go back every hour to trace the shadows again (in different colors of chalk). Watch what happens to the shadows (they start out longer in the morning and gradually shrink as the sun gets higher in the sky).

• Play Shadow Tag! You'll need a sunny day. Students spread out in a sunny area (no shade). The leader tries to tag other students by stepping on their shadows. The person whose shadow is tagged becomes the new leader.

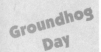

Arts/Crafts Experience

- Students can make their own shadows by folding a piece of light construction paper in half. They paint a self-portrait on one half in dark tempera. When the painting is complete, before it dries, they fold the blank side over the portrait and press gently together.

- Let students make a pop-up groundhog by coloring and cutting out a groundhog pattern (both sides) and stapling it to the top of a straw. They poke a hole in the bottom of a paper cup for the straw to go through. Students can paint or use black marker to draw a "shadow" of the groundhog on the white cup, then glue cotton around the edges of the cup to resemble snow. When the groundhog pops up out of the snow and sees his shadow, he gets scared and pops back down again! See the groundhog patterns on page 16.

- Have each student draw a background picture of land and sky. After cutting a slit 2" in the middle of the land area, they can color and cut out a groundhog from page 16 and mount it on a craft stick to slide the groundhog in and out of the scene.

- Monet was a famous artist who often captured the gradations of light in a day in his paintings. Have students fold art paper in fourths. Take them outside. Have each choose an object to concentrate on and draw, noting particularly where the light falls on it. Take them outside four times during the day to draw. They should record on the bottom of each picture how the light changed throughout the day.

Extension Activities

- Create student "shadow" silhouettes by tracing student profiles. Create the shadows by having students stand very still in front of the light of an overhead projector or slide projector. Trace around the shadows on paper you have attached to the wall.

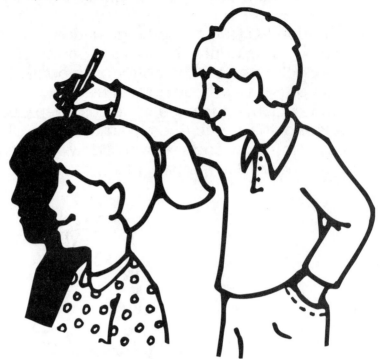

⚠ Make shadow snacks. Using cookie cutters in animal shapes, let students cut two shapes out of soft bread. Then they can spread jam on one side and leave the other plain. They can match up their animal-shaped bread with its shadow likeness and enjoy a "light" snack! (If you prefer, dark-colored cookies with light colored frosting can be found in grocery stores.)

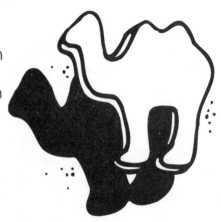

Values Education Experience

- Talk about what it means to "walk in another's shadow." Ask students how they feel about this. What qualities in another person make him or her worth emulating?

Follow-Up/Homework Idea

- Challenge students not to step on their shadows as they walk home today!

I'm Sleeping all Winter!

Name: _____

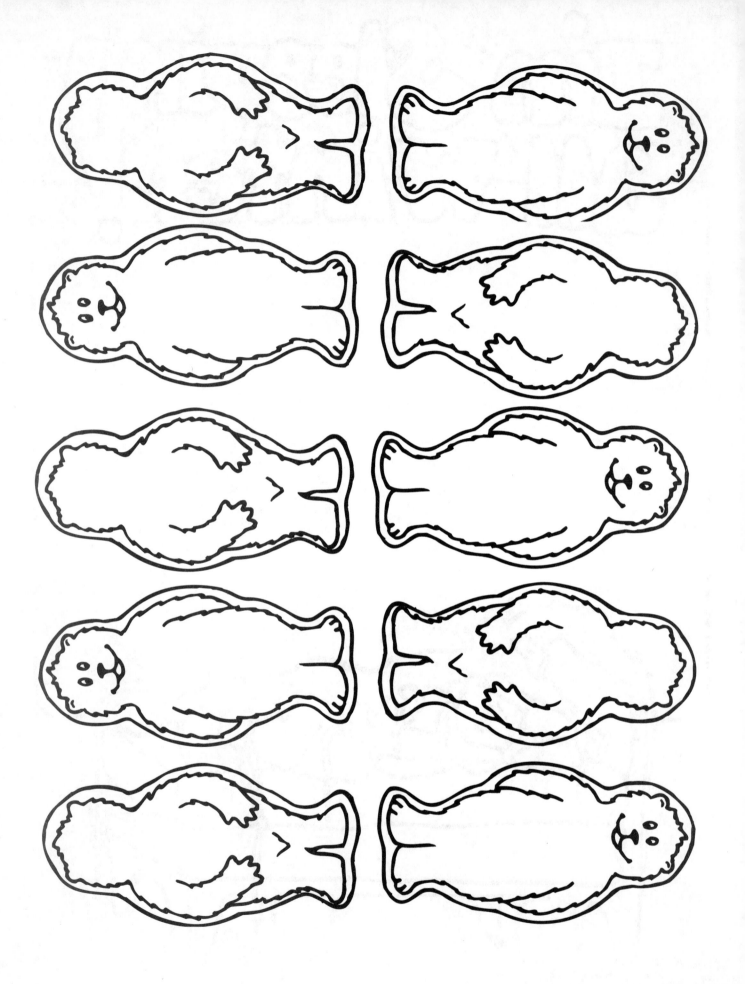

Norman Rockwell's Birthday

February 3

Setting the Stage
- Display Norman Rockwell prints or magazine covers on a table to gather interest in today's activities.

Historical Background
The American illustrator and painter, Norman Rockwell, was born on this day in 1894. He illustrated more than 300 *Saturday Evening Post* magazine covers.

Literary Exploration
Norman Rockwell by Mike Venezia
Norman Rockwell: America's Best-Loved Illustrator by Joel Cohen
Norman Rockwell: The Life of an Artist by Jennifer Rozines Roy
The Norman Rockwell Storybook by Jan Wahl
Norman Rockwell: Storyteller with a Brush by Beverly Gherman
Willie Was Different: A Children's Story by Norman Rockwell

Language Experience

• How many new words can your students make using the letters in *Norman Rockwell*?

• Have one student hold a Rockwell picture so other students cannot see it. He or she describes it as thoroughly as possible and the other students try to draw it. Then compare the drawings with Rockwell's.

Writing Experience

• Gather *Saturday Evening Post* magazine covers or other pictures that Rockwell has done and let students give them titles or captions. Then let each student write a story about what is happening in his or her favorite picture.

Social Studies Experience

• Rockwell's artwork usually exhibits "a slice of American life." He painted pictures of everyday people doing everyday things. Look at some of his pictures and discuss what they show about American life. How might "typical American life" differ from life in other countries?

Music/Dramatic Experience
• Let students choose a Rockwell magazine cover or print and role-play the situation in the picture.

Arts/Crafts Experience
• Let students "capture American life" paintings of their own as Norman Rockwell did.

Extension Activities
⚠ Serve a "slice of life" by giving students all-American apple pie to eat.

Values Education Experience
• Show students Rockwell's pictures of the "Four Freedoms." Discuss the importance of each freedom and how thankful we should be for all of them.

Charles
Lindbergh

Charles
Lindbergh

Charles
Lindbergh

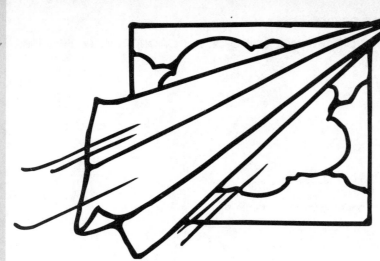

Charles Lindbergh's Birthday

February 4

Setting the Stage

• Today plan on having just "plane" fun! Display all kinds of pictures and books about flying and toy or model airplanes to gather excitement in today's activities.

• Construct a semantic map or web with facts your students already know about airplanes or flight. Then ask them to list questions about airplanes and how they fly today.

Historical Background

Charles Lindbergh was born on this day in 1902. In 1927 he was the first person to fly solo across the Atlantic. It took 33$\frac{1}{2}$ hours to fly from Long Island, New York, to Paris, France.

BORN
1902

Literary Exploration

Airplanes and Flying Machines by Gallimard Jeunesse

Airplanes by Byron Barton

Amelia Earhart: Pioneer of the Sky by John Parlin

Charles Lindbergh by Kenneth G. Richards

Charles Lindbergh, Hero Pilot by David R. Collins

Eureka! It's an Airplane! by Jeanne Bendick

The First Solo Transatlantic Flight: The Story of Charles Lindbergh and His Airplane, the Spirit of St. Louis by Richard L. Taylor

Flight: The Journey of Charles Lindbergh by Robert Burleigh

Fly Away Home by Eve Bunting

Flying (Let's Discover Library) by Patricia Daniels

Granpa Is a Flyer by Sanna Anderson Baker

The Paper Airplane Book by Seymour Simon

Planes by Anne Rockwell

Redbird by Patrick Fort

Richard Scarry's Planes by Richard Scarry

Ruth Law Thrills a Nation by Don Brown

View from the Air: Charles Lindbergh's Earth and Sky by Reeve Lindbergh

The Wright Brothers at Kitty Hawk by Donold J. Sobol

Language Experience

• Play Clothesline (a variation of Hangman). Students try to avoid putting up articles of clothing on a line as they guess the letters of the name of Lindbergh's plane (the *Spirit of St. Louis*).

Writing Experience

• What would Orville and Wilbur Wright think if they could see how far their early invention has come? Invite students to write a conversation between Orville and Wilbur after they take a plane ride today. See patterns on pages 28-29. Let students write on the plane.

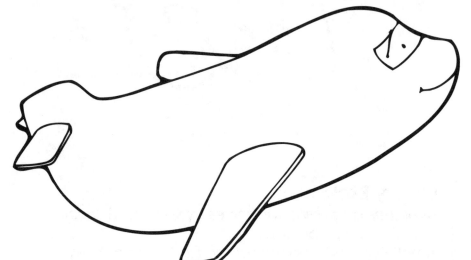

Math Experience

• Designate a "landing field" and let students fly paper airplanes. Measure the distances. Whose plane flew the farthest? Shortest? Most creative (or loopy) flight? Students can try different types of paper airplanes to see which works best.

Science/Health Experience

• Have students study the science of flight to discover how airplanes are able to fly.

Social Studies Experience

• Learn about airplanes and the history of aviation flight. Have students locate important places such as Kitty Hawk, North Carolina, on a map.

Music/Dramatic Experience

⚠ Set up a mock airplane ride (putting chairs in airplane row formation with an aisle). Make airline tickets that can be punched with a hole punch by an "airline attendant." Serve an airline snack and watch a short film on airplanes for an "in-fight" movie.

Physical/Sensory Experience
• Make and fly paper airplanes!

• Blindfold one student at a time to play Pin the Propeller on the Plane (a variation of Pin the Tail on the Donkey). Use the plane patterns on pages 28-29 and the propeller patterns on page 30.

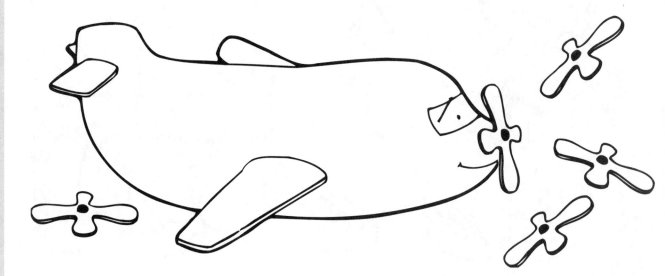

Arts/Crafts Experience

- Make airplanes from craft sticks and hang them in mobiles from the ceiling.

- Let fast finishers work on a mural of an airport and airplanes (leaving plenty of airway strip for landing).

- Have students make flip-top airplanes! Copy the outline of an airplane twice. Let students work on the exterior and interior. Let them look at books for information on the exterior and interior to help with the details. Staple one side of the top of the exterior to the top of the interior so students can "lift" it to see the inside of the plane. See pattern on page 31.

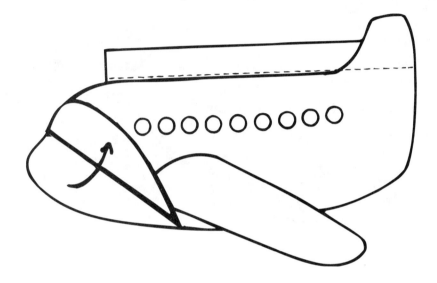

- Students will enjoy naming and designing their own airlines. Let each create a plane. Mount the planes around the room. See if students can guess which airplanes belong to whom. See patterns on pages 28-29.

Extension Activities

⚠ Let students make edible airplanes! They slide a rubber band between two round candy "wheels" (holding on to the ends of the rubber band). They lodge a package of Smarties™ candies or a circus peanut in between the two wheels. The Smarties™ or circus peanut represent the body of the plane. Then they slip both ends of the rubber band over a stick of gum, which represents the wings of the plane.

• Invite an airplane pilot to visit your class and talk about how it feels to fly an airplane.

Extension Activities continued

- If your school is near an airport, get permission to take a field trip there. Your students will love it.

- Procure a large empty refrigerator box (from an appliance store). Let students decorate the outside to look like the exterior of a plane and the inside to look like the cockpit of a plane with dials and panels. Hang puffs of cotton batting outside the windows for a realistic sky-view. Inside the cockpit, place a flashlight and books and "in-flight" magazines about airplanes for students to read. Invite them to "earn their wings" (through finished assignments and good behavior) to gain entrance into the cockpit.

Values Education Experience

- Though students know Lindbergh had public satisfaction from his flying achievements, they may not be aware of the personal grief he and his family suffered at the kidnapping and death of his own son. Talk about how to console those who lose family members to death.

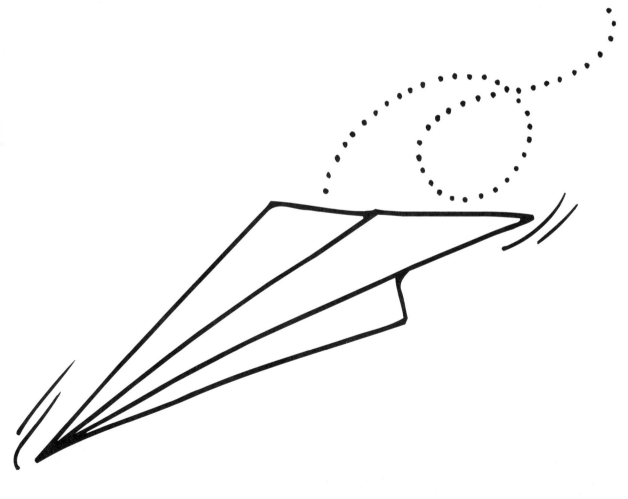

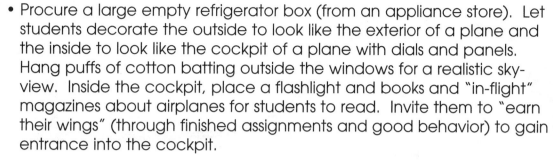

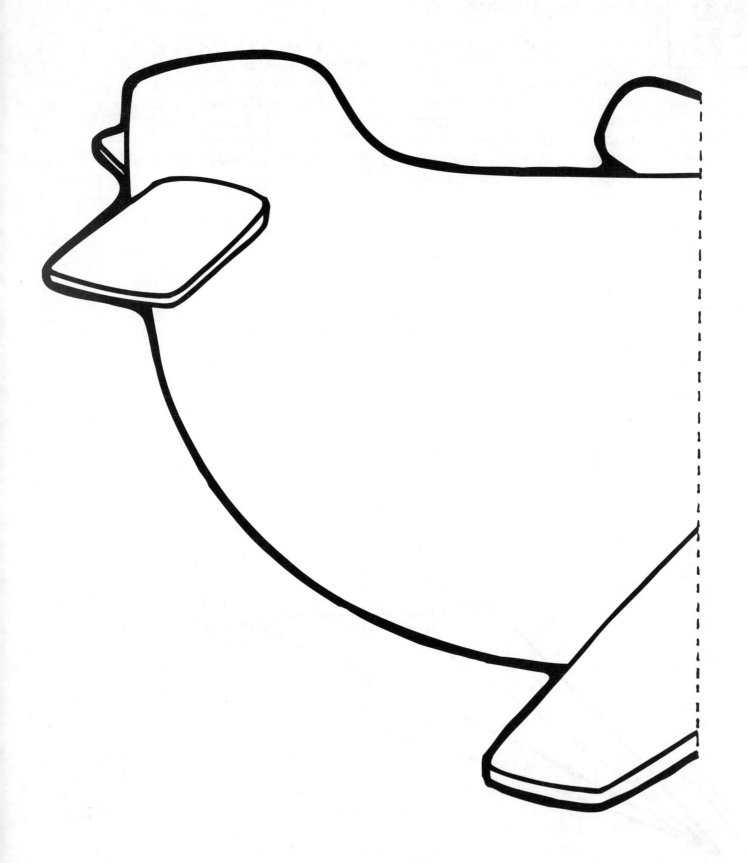

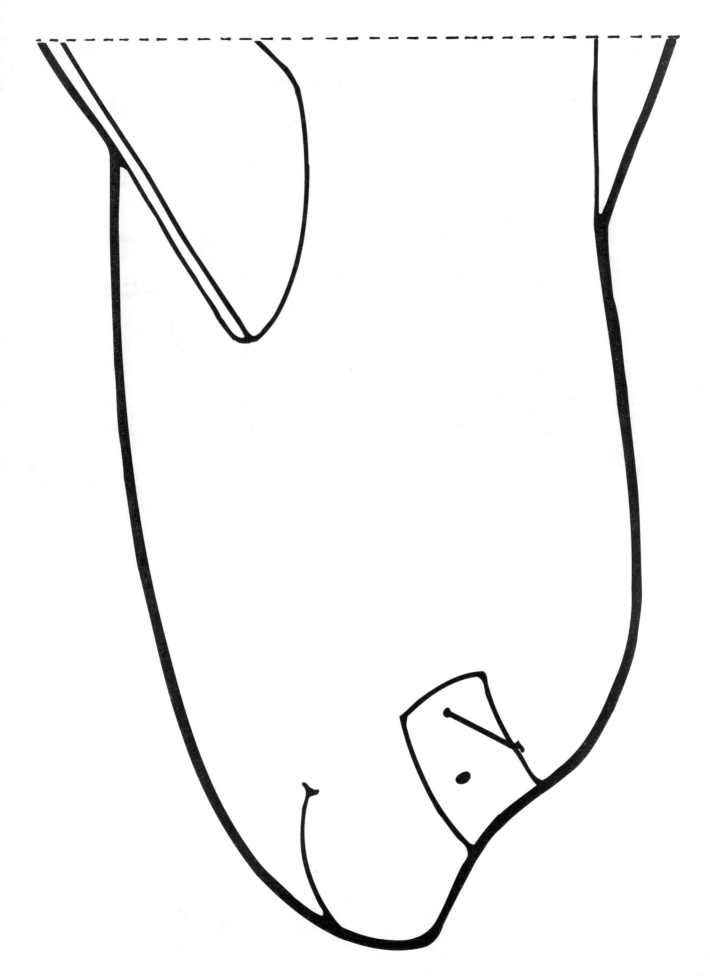

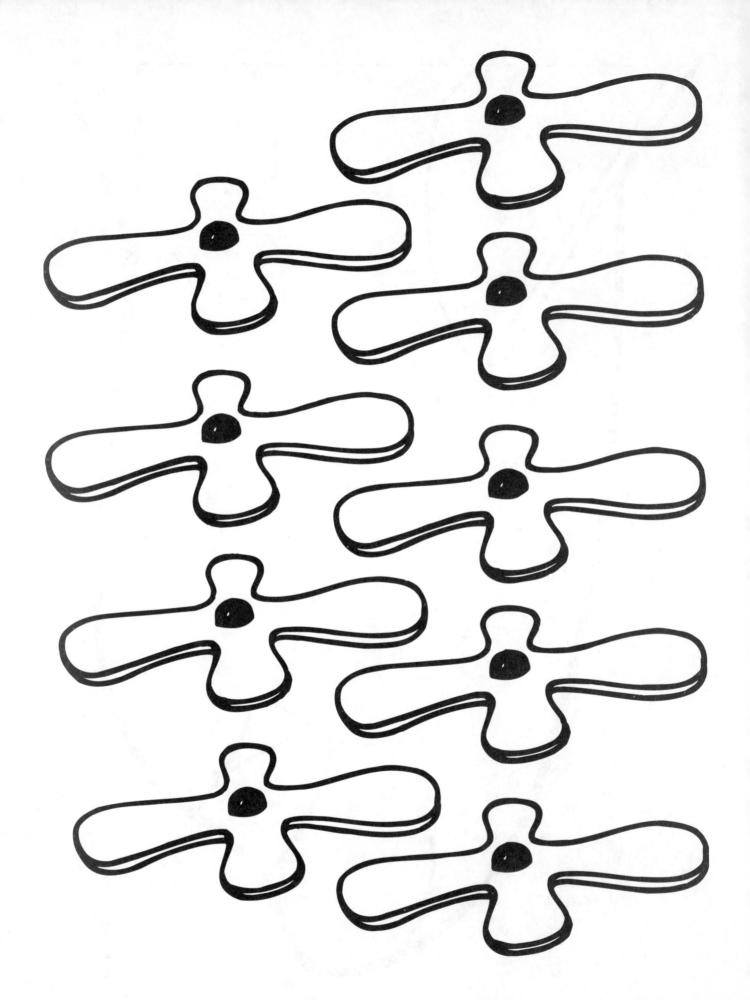

30

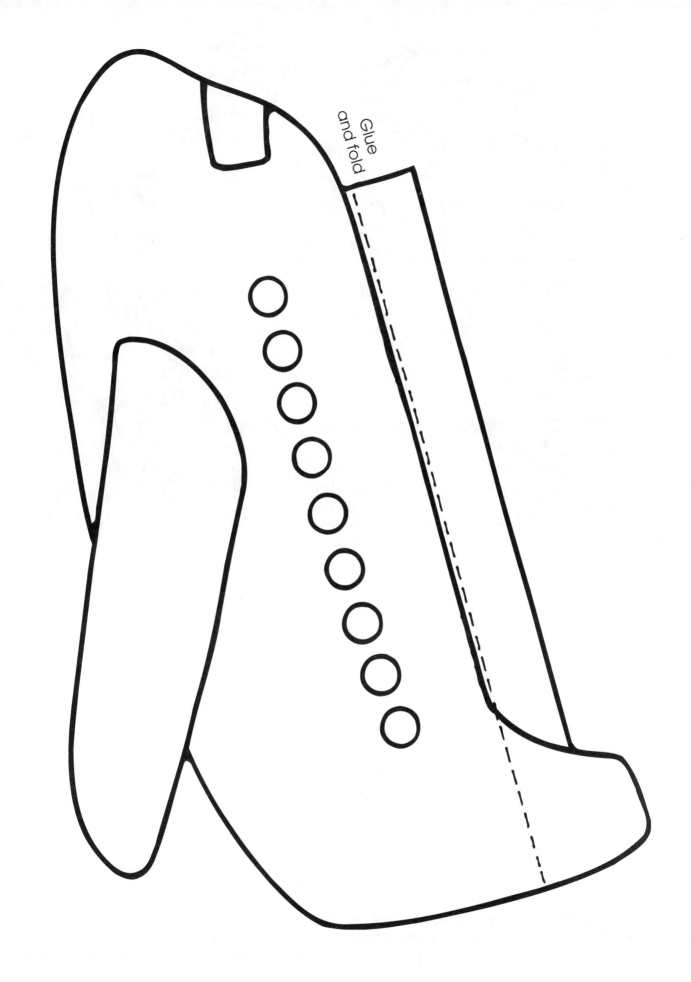

Glue and fold

Blah Buster Day

February 5

Setting the Stage
- Invite students to dress in summer clothes all day to chase the "winter blues" away!

Historical Background
Sometimes at this time of year (after the holidays are over and the weather turns gray and cold) some people seem to experience the "blahs" or "winter blues." "Cabin Fever" is a term used to describe the eagerness people feel to get out after a long time of staying at home because of bad weather.

Literary Exploration
Alexander and the Terrible, Horrible, No Good, Very Bad Day by Judith Viorst
Alicia Has a Bad Day by Lisa Jahn-Clough
Bad Day by Jeni Couzyn
A Bad Week for the Three Bears by Tony Bradman
Bedita's Bad Day by Eros Keith
Benny's Bad Day by Michael Pellowski
Good Days, Bad Days by Catherine Anholt
Horse and the Bad Morning by Theodore Clymer, et al
It Could Always Be Worse by Margot Zemach
That's Good! That's Bad! by Margery Cuyler
Today Was a Terrible Day by Patricia Reilly Giff
Wacky Wednesday by Dr. Suess
"Whatif" a poem from *Where the Sidewalk Ends* by Shel Silverstein
The Wrong Side of the Bed by Wallace E. Keller

Language Experience

• Challenge students to come up with other colorful words to describe the feeling of the "blahs."

• Let students brainstorm things they don't enjoy.

Blah Buster

Blah Buster

Blah Buster

• Review sequencing skills by having students explain the steps they take (in sequence) to change a bad mood to a good mood. (Example: "First, I notice I'm not very happy. Second, I decide I want to change my feelings. Third, I put on some lively music. Fourth, I think of a happy moment.")

• Point out that words can be very helpful and encouraging. Have students think of things to say to one another to build each other up and keep each other from the "blahs." Let them practice saying these words to one another to turn a bad day into a good day.

Blah Buster

Blah Buster

Blah Buster

Blah Buster

Writing Experience

• Share an experience when you have had a "terrible, horrible, no good, very bad day." Invite students to write stories about their own "terrible, horrible, no good very bad days. See reproducible on page 38.

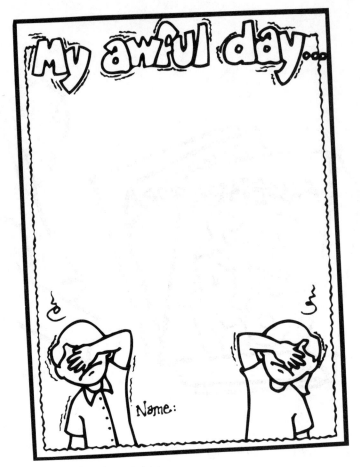

• Have students write their feelings using these story starters:

> I don't like it when . . .
> Once, I . . .
> What really bothers me is . . .
> I wish people would not . . .
> I could do without . . .
> It really makes me grouchy when . . .
> It really bugs me when . . .

• Let each student write a scenario for an awful day, followed by a scenario for a perfect day!

34

Science/Health Experience

• Students may not realize that they have the power to be in charge of their own feelings. They can learn how to change a bad mood into a good mood. Review steps they can take to change their attitudes when they are not feeling their best.

Social Studies Experience

• When people feel blue or "blah," they can turn their feelings around through acts of kindness and service to others. Talk about how doing kind things for others gives us an emotional lift that helps chase away blue feelings. Encourage students to be kinder the worse they feel! Their feeling will improve.

Music/Dramatic Experience

• Have students role-play situations of problems or mistakes that are "turned around" into positive learning experiences.

When life gives you lemons....

Lila's fresh LEMONADE
10¢ Coldest & Sweetest in town!

Blah Buster

Blah Buster

Blah Buster

Physical/Sensory Experience

• Explain that fresh air and exercise is a good prescription to chase away the winter blues. Run around the school or do some simple warm-up exercises together.

Arts/Crafts Experience

• Let students paint to chase the "blues" away as they listen to upbeat music.

• Let students illustrate "from bad to worse" experiences.

• Have students cut out magazine pictures of things that make them happy (or of happy faces) to make collages.

Blah Buster

Blah Buster

Blah Buster

36

Extension Activities

⚠ After reading *Alexander and the Terrible, Horrible, No Good, Very Bad Day* by Judith Viorst, the class can make cupcakes (or some other treat) for others who didn't get what they wanted in their lunch boxes.

Follow-Up/Homework Idea

• Challenge students to be "thermostats" not "thermometers." Thermometers "read" the temperature around them but thermostats "set" the temperature. Students can match the mood around them or set their own good mood and influence others to be happy.

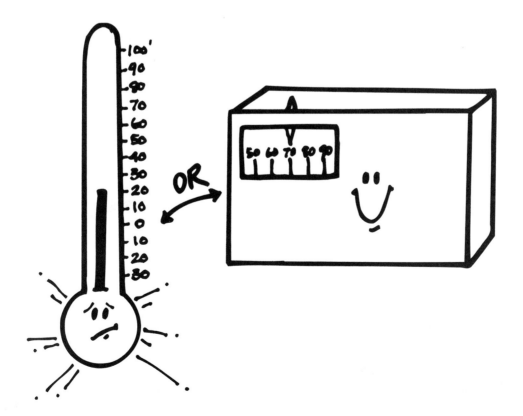

Ronald Reagan's Birthday

February 6

Historical Background

Ronald Reagan, the 40th President of the United States, was born on this day in 1911.

Literary Exploration

The Picture Life of Ronald Reagan by Don Lawson
Ronald Reagan by Zachary Kent
Ronald Reagan by George Sullivan
Ronald Reagan, an All American by June Behrens
Ronald Reagan, 40th President of the United States by Neal E. Robbins
Ronald Reagan, President by John Devaney

Language Experience

• How many new words can your students make using the letters in *Ronald Reagan*?

Writing Experience
• Reagan was President during the 1980s, which came to be known as the ME decade. Many books were written about how to get ahead and looking out for #1. Ask students to write their feelings about what kind of world we would live in if everyone only looked out for himself or herself. See reproducible on page 42.

Name:

Math Experience
• Ronald Reagan was the oldest man ever-elected President. He was born on this day in 1911. How old would he be today?

Social Studies Experience
• Study the life and presidency of Ronald Reagan.

Music/Dramatic Experience

- Students may not be aware that Reagan was a movie star in more than 50 films before he ever became President of the United States. What on-stage skills probably helped him in politics?

Enthusiasm

Soberness

Confidence

- Check out one of Ronald Reagan's films from the library and have students watch.

Extension Activities

⚠ Reagan loved jellybeans and kept some on his desk all the time. Serve jellybeans in honor of Ronald Reagan today!

Follow-Up/Homework Idea

- Encourage students to ask their parents what they remember about President Ronald Reagan.

Ronald Reagan

Ronald Reagan

Ronald Reagan

Name:

Laura Ingalls Wilder's Birthday

February 7

Setting the Stage

- Display items, books and pictures related to frontier life on the prairie. Include Laura Ingalls Wilder's "Little House" series of books.

- Construct a semantic map or web with facts your students already know (or would like to know) about frontier or prairie life.

Historical Background

American author, Laura Ingalls Wilder, was born on this day in 1867.

Laura
Ingalls
Wilder

Laura
Ingalls
Wilder

Laura
Ingalls
Wilder

Literary Exploration

By the Shores of Silver Lake by Laura Ingalls Wilder
Farmer Boy by Laura Ingalls Wilder
Laura Ingalls Wilder by Gwenda Blair
Laura Ingalls Wilder by Jill C. Wheeler
Laura Ingalls Wilder: Author of the Little House Books by Carol Greene
Laura Ingalls Wilder: A Biography by William Anderson
Laura Ingalls Wilder Country Cookbook by Laura Ingalls Wilder, et al
Laura Ingalls Wilder: Growing up in the Little House by Patricia Reilly Giff
Laura: The Life of Laura Ingalls Wilder by Donald Zochert
Laura Ingalls Wilder Songbook by Eugenia Garson
Little House (series) by Laura Ingalls Wilder
Little House in the Big Woods by Laura Ingalls Wilder
The Long Winter by Laura Ingalls Wilder
On the Banks of Plum Creek by Laura Ingalls Wilder
Story of Laura Ingalls Wilder, Pioneer Girl by Megan Stine
These Happy Golden Years by Laura Ingalls Wilder
Winter Days in the Big Woods by Laura Ingalls Wilder
Winter on the Farm by Laura Ingalls Wilder

Language Experience

- Create a Venn diagram depicting the differences and similarities between life now and life in "Wilder" times!

Writing Experience

- Have students write (as Laura Ingalls Wilder did) about their everyday family lives. See reproducible on page 47.

All about my family...

Name:

Social Studies Experience

- Learn what life was like (homes, food, clothes, games, chores and recreation) in Middle America during the late 1800s.

- Read aloud from: *Laura: The Life of Laura Ingalls Wilder* by Donald Zochert or *Laura Ingalls Wilder: Growing up in the Little House* by Patricia Reilly Giff to help students understand something about the experiences of Laura Ingalls Wilder.

Music/Dramatic Experience

- Choose songs out of the *Laura Ingalls Wilder Songbook* by Eugenia Garson to sing with your class.

Physical/Sensory Experience

- Play a few favorite games from the "old days" such as Hide and Seek or Kick the Can.

Arts/Crafts Experience

• Students can illustrate a scene from one of Wilder's books on a mural or create a diorama.

Extension Activities

⚠ Choose a fun recipe for students to make from the *Laura Ingalls Wilder Country Cookbook* by Laura Ingalls Wilder. Try a prairie favorite such as beef jerky or honey on cornbread.

Values Education Experience

• Some people think they are too young or old to begin something that they want to do. Laura Ingalls Wilder began writing her famous book series when she was 65 years old! Her daughter, Rose Wilder Lane, flew over San Francisco Bay strapped to the wing of an airplane at the age of 78! Encourage students to follow their dreams and not let age (or anything else) limit them!

Follow-Up/Homework Idea

• Encourage students to check out Laura Ingalls Wilder's books from the library to begin reading at home.

46

All about my family...

Name:

Futuristic Day

February 8

Setting the Stage

• Display pictures and items that would have been "futuristic" in Jules Verne's day. He wrote about things not in existence at the time but later became real inventions (submarines, television, space ships, rockets and missiles, dirigibles, air conditioners and even the remote control).

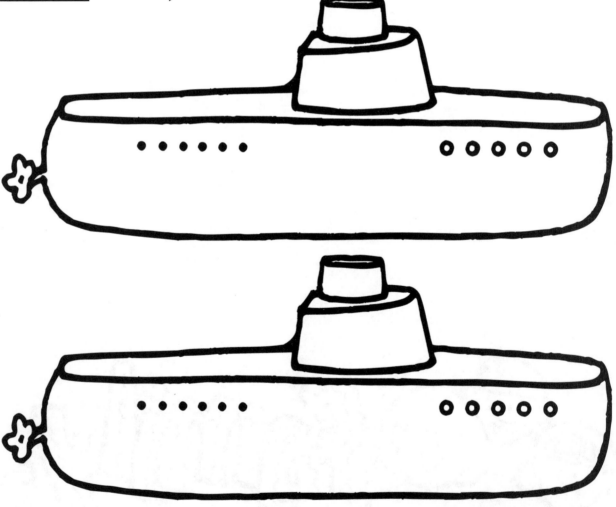

• Construct a semantic map or web with ideas your students think of when they think of the future. What questions do they have about the future?

48

Historical Background

Jules Verne was a science fiction writer born in France on this day in 1828. He is known for thinking "ahead of his time." He had a rare talent of combining scientific fact with fantasy that resulted in great science fiction stories.

Literary Exploration

Around the World in Eighty Days by Jules Verne
From the Earth to the Moon by Jules Verne
FutureWorld by John Ryder Hall
Jules Verne by Beril Becker
Jules Verne: The Man Who Invented the Future by Franz Born
Round the Moon by Jules Verne
"Submarines" an excerpt from *I Wonder Why the Sea Is Salty and Other Questions About the Oceans* by Anita Ganeri
Who Said There's No Man on the Moon? by Robert Quackenbush
Wilbur's Space Machine by Lorna Balian

Language Experience

• Challenge students to think of words that rhyme with *Verne*. (*learn, turn, adjourn, churn*)

Writing Experience

• Let students predict what they think the world will be like in the future, then write about it using descriptive imagery. See reproducible on page 52.

In the Future

Name:

Futuristic

Futuristic

Futuristic

Math Experience

• Jules Verne wrote about a ship that could go under the sea (an idea that seemed preposterous at the time) but later proved possible with the birth of the submarine. Write "sub"traction problems on submarine shapes for students to solve. Copy the submarine art on page 48.

Science/Health Experience

• Let students suggest possible future developments in science and health.

• Let students discover how a periscope works. They can help you make a periscope (a great addition to a classroom submarine) by cutting two windows across from two tilted mirrors. The mirrors are placed in opposite corners (one on top and one on bottom). Test to see if the periscope is working properly by looking into the bottom hole to see out of the top hole.

Social Studies Experience

• Challenge students to make predictions about travel, food, technology or amusement in the future, such as 50 or 100 years from now.

• Let students research biographical information about Jules Verne and share the information with the class.

Arts/Crafts Experience

• Let students create or design futuristic space vehicles or playgrounds. They can draw their designs on paper or make scale models of them.

Extension Activities

• Get a refrigerator box from an appliance store to create a class "submarine." Decorate it inside and out to resemble a submarine (using details found in books). Over the windows, hang dangling fish and sea creatures for the "submarine" observers inside. Inside the submarine, place literature about the future such as Jules Verne's books.

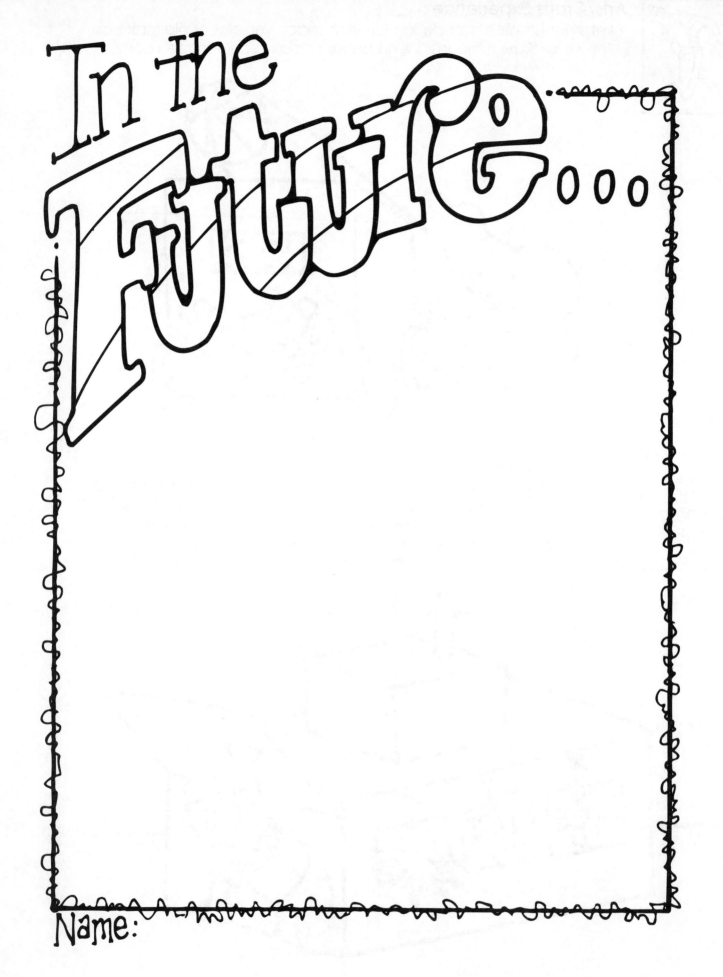

In the Future...

Name:

Weather Service Day

February 9

Setting the Stage

- Display weather-tracking and measurement devices (thermometer, barometer, etc.) next to an umbrella, mittens and woolen cap, and a beach ball!

- Create a large weather calendar on which students can place weather symbol cut-outs. You may draw it on the board and let students tape symbol cut-outs directly to the board for an ongoing center. Use the patterns on page 60.

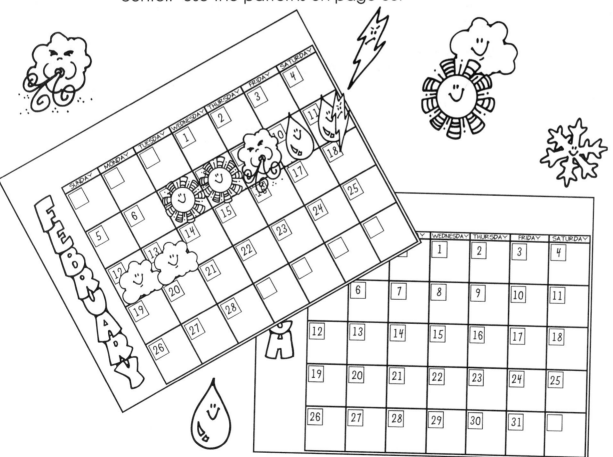

- Construct a semantic map or web with facts your students already know about weather. Then have them list questions they want answers to.

Weather
Service

Weather
Service

Weather
Service

Historical Background

The U.S. Government (Congress) established the National Weather Service on this day in 1870.

National Weather Service since 1870.

Literary Exploration

Bear Weather by Lillie Chaffin
The Big Storm by Bruce Hiscock
Boot Weather by Judith Vigna
Chinook! by Michael O. Tunnell
Dorrie and the Weather Box by Patricia Coombs
Earth Weather as Explained by Professor Xargle by Jeanne Willis
Flash, Crash, Rumble and Roll by Franklyn M. Branley
Forecast by Malcolm Hall
Hurricane by David Wiesner
I Like Weather by Aileen Fisher
It's Raining Cats and Dogs: All Kinds of Weather and Why We Have It by
    Franklyn M. Branley
Kipper's Book of Weather by Mick Inkpen
Questions and Answers About Weather by Jean M. Craig
Rain and Hail by Franklyn M. Branley
The Storm Book by Charlotte Zolotow
Storms by Seymour Simon
Stormy Weather by Amanda Harvey
Sun Up by Alvin Tresselt
Thunder Cake by Patricia Polacco
Weather by David Lambert
Weather by Jan Pienkowski
Weather by Seymour Simon
Weather and Climate by Barbara Taylor
Weather Forecasting by Gail Gibbons
Weather: Poems for All Seasons by Lee Bennett Hopkins
Weather Report: Poems by Jane Yolen
Weather Words and What They Mean by Gail Gibbons
The Weeds and the Weather by Mary Stolz
What Makes the Weather by Janet Palazzo
What Will the Weather Be? by Lynda DeWitt
What Will the Weather Be Like Today? by Paul Rogers
What's the Weather Today? by Allan Fowler
The World of Weather by Robin Kerrod

Language Experience
- Brainstorm weather words together. (storm, blizzard, hail, sleet, thunder, lightning, sunny, foggy, frost, windy, tornado, rain, fog, ice, cloudy, dew, mist, breezy, rainbow, drizzling, hurricane)

Writing Experience
- Have students write about the kind of weather they like best and explain why. See reproducible on page 61.

- Students will enjoy writing weather legends, such as: what causes thunder and lightning or what makes the wind blow?

Math Experience

• Begin tracking the weather, marking down specific types of weather on a bar graph (such as five rainy days). Keep a thermometer outside a school window and graph daily temperatures. See reproducible on page 62.

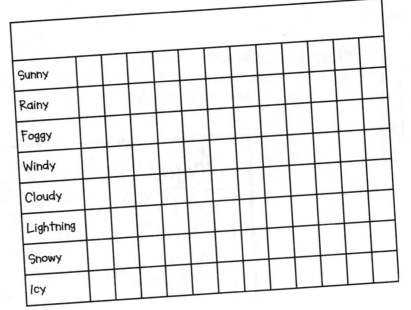

Sunny												
Rainy												
Foggy												
Windy												
Cloudy												
Lightning												
Snowy												
Icy												

• Review probability with your students. Encourage them to predict what the weather will be like over the next week, then figure the probability of each type of weather. Have students record the actual weather conditions during the week to compare with their predictions.

Science/Health Experience

• Begin a unit on weather! Review weather safety (lightning, tornadoes, flooding, etc.).

Social Studies Experience

- Throughout history, people have gained information on the weather in many ways, from changes in animal behavior and reading almanacs to sophisticated instruments. Let students research how weather forecasting methods have changed over the years.

Music/Dramatic Experience

- Sing "The Weather Song" written by Linda Kaman from the songbook, *More Piggyback Songs*.

- If you have a dramatic play area, let students dress for certain types of weather (raincoat and umbrella or mittens and heavy coat and hat).

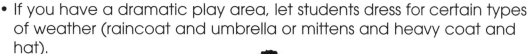

Physical/Sensory Experience

- Involve students in weather creative dance! With background music (including drums or rhythm instruments), let students pretend to create rain, snow, wind, thunder, etc., with their bodies.

- Play Jack Frost Tag! Assign one student to be Jack Frost and one to be Jane Thaw. Students try to avoid getting tagged. If tagged, they are "frozen." Only Jane Thaw can unfreeze or "thaw" students to play in the game again.

Arts/Crafts Experience

- Tack a large piece of butcher paper on one wall and add the caption: "Weather Center." Label the following columns: *Rainy Day, Sunny Day, Snowy Day, Stormy Day, Tornado Day* and *Windy Day*. Have students cut out newspaper articles and pictures they draw or cut out of magazines that correlate the type of weather which they caption and add them to the chart.

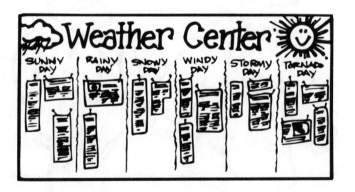

Extension Activities

- Visit a weather station if there's one nearby.

- Invite a weather forecaster or meteorologist to come to your class and talk about his or her work.

Follow-Up/Homework Idea

- Tell students to watch a weather report on television or read the weather report from a newspaper. They should be ready to share it with the class. Compare weather reports from various sources.

My favorite kind of Weather...

Name:

	Sunny	Rainy	Foggy	Windy	Cloudy	Lightning	Snowy	Icy

Singing Telegram Day

February 10

Singing
Telegram

Singing
Telegram

Singing
Telegram

Setting the Stage
- Begin the day with a personalized singing telegram to grab everyone's attention. Ask a local telegram company to donate their services or invite another adult in the school to come and sing it to your class.

Historical Background
The first singing telegram was delivered in New York City on this day in 1933.

Singing
Telegram

Language Experience
- How many new words can your students make using the letters in *singing telegram*?

 ### Writing Experience
- Let students (individually or together) create a singing telegram to a familiar tune. See reproducible on page 65.

See reproducible on page 65.

 ### Social Studies Experience
- Invite interested students to research the history of telegrams and share that information with the class.

 ### Music/Dramatic Experience
- Your students can create and perform their telegrams for the class or others such as the school librarian, secretary or nurse.

 ### Arts/Crafts Experience
- Let students decorate the borders of their singing telegrams.

- Students may design silly costumes to wear when they sing their telegrams.

 ### Extension Activities
- Contact a local representative from a singing telegram company to talk about his or her work.

 ### Values Education Experience
- Discuss the importance of lyrics in students' singing telegrams that encourage and cheer those who receive them.

Thomas Edison's Birthday

February 11

Setting the Stage

- Display "inventions" (can opener, straw, tape dispenser, staple remover, thumbtack, etc.) around a light bulb with the caption: "Bright Ideas!"

- Dress like an inventor, wearing a white lab coat. Hold a notebook in your hand and wear glasses.

- Construct a semantic web with facts your students already know about inventions and inventors. Invite them to write questions they want answered.

Historical Background

Thomas Edison was a famous American inventor born on this day in 1847.

Literary Exploration

Almost Famous by David Getz

Be an Inventor by Barbara Taylor

Dreamers and Doers: Inventors Who Changed the World by Norman Richards

Extraordinary Stories Behind the Invention of Ordinary Things by Don L. Wulffson

How to Be an Inventor by Harvey Weiss

I Gave Thomas Edison My Sandwich by Floyd C. Moore

Invention (Eyewitness Books) by Lionel Bender

Invention Book by Steven Caney

Inventions by Ian Graham

The Inventors by Nathan Aaseng

Inventors and Inventions by Michael Jeffries and Gary Lewis

Mistakes That Worked by Charlotte Foltz Jones

Mothers of Invention by Ethlie Vare

The Picture History of the Great Inventors by Gillian Clements

Small Inventions That Make a Big Difference by National Geographic Society and Donald J. Crump

1000 Inventions by Alan Benjamin

The Story of Thomas Alva Edison by Margaret Cousins

The Story of Thomas Alva Edison by Margaret Davidson

Thomas Alva Edison by Vincent Buranelli

Thomas Alva Edison: Young Inventor by Louis Sabin

Thomas Edison by Nina Morgan

Thomas Edison: The Great American Inventor by Louise Egan

Thomas Edison: Inventing the Future by Penny Mintz

The Value of Creativity: The Story of Thomas Edison by Ann Johnson

Weird and Wacky Inventions by Jim Murphy

What If? Fifty Discoveries That Changed the World by Seli Groves and Dian Buchman

The World Almanac Book of Inventions by Valerie-Anne Giscard d'Estaing

Thomas Edison

Thomas Edison

Thomas Edison

Language Experience

- Have students brainstorm new inventions in the past 20 years (DVDs, car air bags, etc.), then list them in alphabetical order. Have them look in dictionaries to see how many of the new words are listed.

Writing Experience

- Get students thinking about problems that need to be solved. These may include things that really bug them or things they wish would or would not happen. (Example: sunglasses with little windshield wipers for when it rains) Have them write their wishes down, then write about some ways to solve the problems. They may give their solutions or "inventions" names.

  Problem + Time / Thought = Solution / Invention

- Ask students to write how they would feel if they invented something that turned out to be important to mankind. See reproducible on page 72.

Science/Health Experience

• Walter Hunt invented the safety pin. This is a great day to begin a unit of study on inventions, small and large.

Social Studies Experience

• Invite students to research Edison and share their findings with the class. They might not be aware that Edison had over 1200 different inventions, including: the light bulb, phonograph, movie projector, storage battery, ticker tape machine, typewriter and mimeograph machine. The invention that Thomas Edison is most famous for, the light bulb, was not actually his invention. He perfected one that had already been made by Humphrey Davey and Joseph Swan. Edison tried over 6000 different ideas before finding the right filament to burn in a light bulb. It was Thomas Edison who brought this important discovery to "light" so others could benefit from its use.

• Have students research other great inventors throughout history: Samuel Morse, Eli Whitney, Elias Howe, Alexander Graham Bell. They can create a time line depicting important inventions. Have them write summaries about the inventors on a light bulb shape and display them on a bulletin board. See light bulb patterns on page 73.

Music/Dramatic Experience
• Let students "advertise" their new inventions to "interested buyers" in your class!

Physical/Sensory Experience
• Divide the class into cooperative groups. Provide a variety of objects to each group. Challenge them to put the items together in a new way. They'll need to brainstorm new inventions and explain to the class what their function is and how they might be useful to others.

Arts/Crafts Experience
• Before actually making their inventions, be sure students illustrate their plans (with labels) on a blueprint.

70

Extension Activities

• Invite an inventor to your class to talk about his or her work.

• Serve Popsicles™! An 11-year old boy inadvertently left a stirring stick in his soda water overnight where it froze. Presto! The invention of the Popsicle™! He later opened a business selling Popsicles™ for which boys and girls are grateful today!

• Host an Invention Convention! All class inventors can share their inventions with the class or with other classes!

Values Education Experience

• Edison had a great work ethic! He said his success was due to "1% inspiration and 99% perspiration!" "I never did anything worth doing by accident, nor did any of my inventions come by accident, they came by work," Edison said. Discuss the value of hard work for success.

Follow-Up/Homework Idea

• Encourage students to save electricity by making sure all the lights are turned off in unused rooms at home.

72

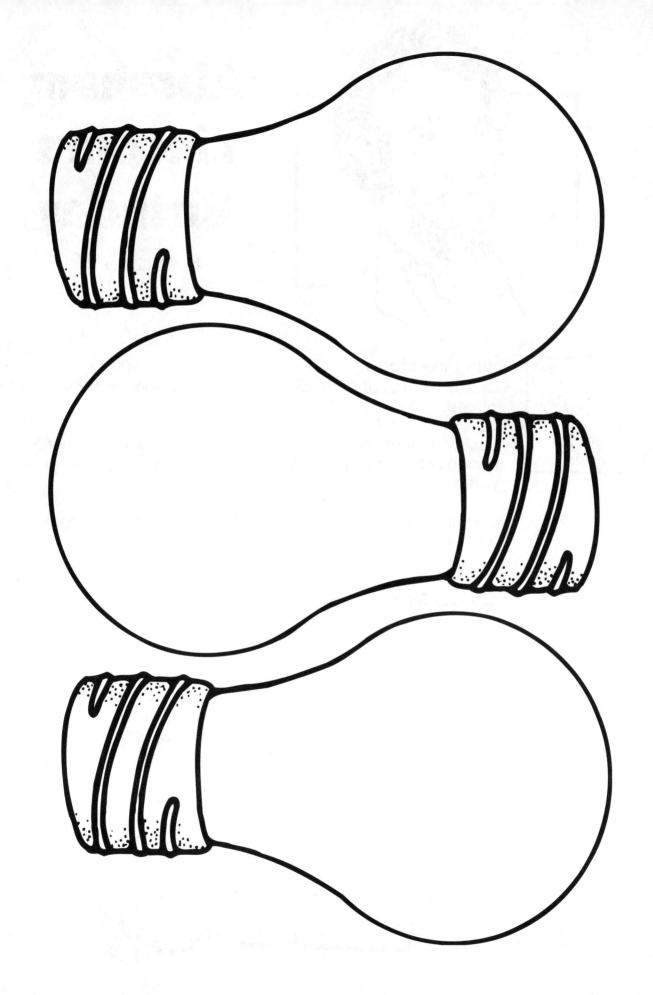

Abraham Lincoln's Birthday

February 12

Setting the Stage

• Display pictures of Abraham Lincoln with related literature to invite interest.

• Display student silhouettes (facial profiles on black construction paper) around the silhouettes of Abraham Lincoln and George Washington with the caption: "Great Americans."

• Construct a semantic web with facts students already know (or would like to know) about Abraham Lincoln.

Historical Background

Abraham Lincoln, born on this day in 1809, grew up to be the 16th President of the United States.

TLC10467 Copyright © Teaching & Learning Company, Carthage, IL 62321-0010

Literary Exploration

Abe Lincoln's Hat by Martha Brenner
Abraham Lincoln by Anne Colver
Abraham Lincoln by Ingri and Edgar Parin d'Aulair
Abraham Lincoln, Friend of the People by Clara Ingram Judson
The Abraham Lincoln Joke Book by Beatrice Schenck de Regniers
Abraham Lincoln, President for the People by Larry Weinberg
Honest Abe by Edith Kunhardt
If You Grew up with Abraham Lincoln by Ann McGovern
Just a Few Words, Mr. Lincoln: The Story of the Gettysburg Address by
    Jean Fritz
Just Like Abraham Lincoln by Bernard Waber
Let's Find Out About Abraham Lincoln by Martha and Charles Shapp
Lincoln: A Photobiography by Russell Freedman
Lincoln's Birthday by Dennis Fradin
Lincoln's Little Girl: A True Story by Fred Trump
Me and Willie and Pa: The Story of Abraham Lincoln and His Son Tad
    by Ferdinand Monjo
Meet Abraham Lincoln by Barbara Cary
Mr. Lincoln's Whiskers by Karen B. Winnick
A Picture Book of Abraham Lincoln by David A. Adler
The Story of the Lincoln Memorial by Natalie Miller
True Stories About Abraham Lincoln by Ruth Belov Gross

Language Experience

- Create a Venn diagram depicting the similarities and differences between Abraham Lincoln and George Washington.

Abraham
Lincoln

Abraham
Lincoln

Abraham
Lincoln

Writing Experience

• Most students admire Lincoln because of the stories that have been told about him. Lincoln had an easy manner with young children and they felt they could approach him. One 11-year-old girl suggested he wear a beard. He was not offended, but took her suggestion right away. His beard became one of his trademarks. Do your students have questions they would like to ask Lincoln? Have each one write a letter to him as if he were a friend. They should begin it with: "Dear President Abe Lincoln." See reproducible on page 81.

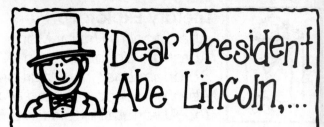

Dear President Abe Lincoln,...

Math Experience

• Who is on both the penny and the five-dollar bill? Gather enough pennies for each student to have one. Let them make coin rubbings. They can review counting, adding or subtracting with the coin rubbings. They may also create math story problems. ("Sarah had 12 pennies and she spent 7. How many does she have left?" or "I have three 5 dollar bills. How much money do I have?")

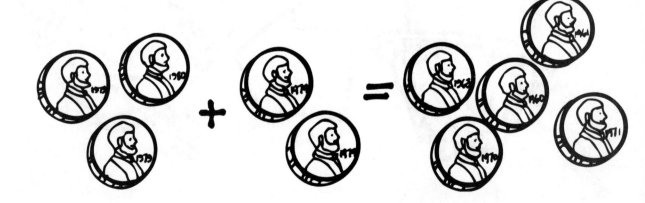

Social Studies Experience

• Study the life and presidency of Abraham Lincoln. Interested students can do extra research for biographical information to share with the rest of the class.

Music/Dramatic Experience

• Give students opportunity to practice situations that put their honesty to the test. Let them act out what they would do in role-play situations involving honesty. (Example: A student finds a watch on the playground. What are some choices that he or she has?)

Physical/Sensory Experience

• Let students construct log cabins with Lincoln Logs.™

• Lincoln loved to read by the fire or candlelight in the evening. Simulate this situation for students by darkening your room and reading to them by candlelight.

Arts/Crafts Experience

6'4" →

• Create a life-sized Lincoln! You'll need butcher paper at least 6'4" long because that's how tall he was! (Be sure to allow even more paper for a hat!) Mark off approximate marks for the starting point to guide students as they draw the head, torso, arms and legs. Let them fill in the rest with paint or markers (looking at books and pictures for details). Trace around the body on a second piece of paper, then staple the two pieces together and stuff them for a three-dimensional effect. Have Lincoln "sit" with your class as they learn about him.

• Let students trace a pattern of Lincoln's profile on black construction paper. Cut out the profile, then cut it into several puzzle pieces. They can trade puzzles with one another and attempt to re-assemble the silhouettes.

Arts/Crafts Experience continued

• Students can make mini log cabins with their milk cartons saved from lunch. Rinse out and dry the milk cartons. Close the pour spout. Glue stick pretzels to the sides and top of the milk carton with thick white frosting. Another kind of log cabin can be made by gluing brown construction paper to the milk carton sides and a brown paper roof stapled on top. Draw stripes with a black marker for logs. A hole can be cut in the top of the roof and a rolled black paper chimney inserted.

Extension Activities

⚠ Make edible log cabins! Give each student a peanut butter sandwich. They cut through the sandwich (four strips lengthwise), then stack the strips end to end into a log cabin. Dribble whipped honey on top to resemble snow.

⚠ Students might enjoy making log cabins out of pretzels and round cereal held together with thick white frosting.

Extension Activities continued

• Try this log cabin idea. Collect toilet paper and paper towel tubes. Lay six long tubes (gift wrap rolls work well) for the "foundation." Then students can glue layer after layer of cardboard tubes to build up the walls. Students will need to glue tubes at right angles to form corners. Challenge them to find a way to put smaller tubes together to make a window and door for the cabin. With everyone working together, you'll soon have a log cabin to be proud of!

Abraham Lincoln

Values Education Experience

• Discuss some of Abraham Lincoln's strengths (honesty, integrity). Have students write about why those qualities are important for everyone to have.

Abraham Lincoln

Follow-Up/Homework Idea

• Encourage students to be honest with their families.

Abraham Lincoln

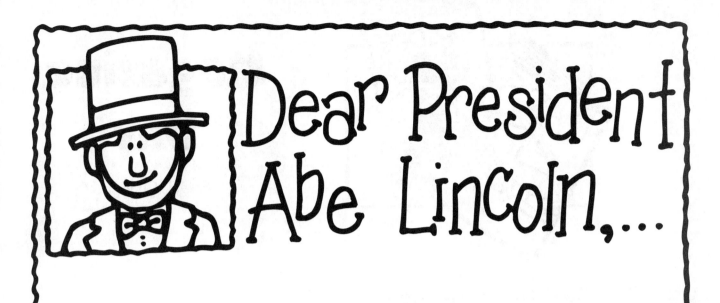

Dear President
Abe Lincoln,...

Magazine Day

February 13

Setting the Stage

- Display different kinds of magazines from various interest groups (sports, fashion, cars, travel, entertainment, etc.).

- Construct a semantic web with facts your students already know (or would like to know) about magazines.

Historical Background

The first magazine in America (*The American Magazine*) was published on this day in 1741, in Philadelphia, Pennsylvania. Contrary to its editor's opinion that it would be what the public wanted, it folded after just three issues.

82

Literary Exploration
• Provide a variety of magazines for students to look through and read.

Language Experience
• Divide students into cooperative groups. Have them find unfamiliar words in magazines, list them and look up their definitions in a dictionary.

• Provide magazines from which students can cut letters of different sizes, fonts and colors. They can use these letters to make words, then complete sentences.

Writing Experience
• Have students cut out pictures of people or animals from magazines, then give them thoughts or words as in a comic strip. See bubble patterns on page 87.

Math Experience

• Create a class bar graph of students' favorite magazines or magazine features (advertisements, sports articles, etc.).

Science/Health Experience

• Let students scour magazines for health-related articles or advertisements which students can share. (Example: This soda pop may be disruptive to your digestive system and can cause severe burping.)

Social Studies Experience

• Follow the history of magazines from their beginning to current use. Discuss how they have changed over the years. Which did early magazines have more of—words or pictures? What do today's magazines have more of?

Music/Dramatic Experience

• Let students present advertisements for certain types of magazines.

Physical/Sensory Experience

• Stage a scavenger hunt and have cooperative groups look for certain things in magazines: a cosmetic advertisement, a word that ends in "ing," a person with a hat and so on.

Arts/Crafts Experience

• Students can cut pictures from magazines and mount them on light cardboard (such as from cereal boxes). Then they can cut the pictures in pieces to create puzzles for other students to put together.

• Create Magazine Montages! Students cut pictures of people or animal body parts (or facial parts) from magazines. Then they put them together in new ways. (Example: the head of a man, the neck of a giraffe, the body of an older woman, the legs of a kitten, the feet of a bird and so on. A face may have different eyes, ears, nose and mouth from various sources.) Students will have fun with this and will be eager to share their final work!

Arts/Crafts Experience continued

• Here's a fun lesson in symmetry! Students cut magazine pictures in half (vertically, down the center) and mount them on art paper. Then they attempt to draw the matching half on the other side.

Extension Activities

• Create a classroom magazine with feature articles, advertisements, pictures, etc., written by students. Keep it in the classroom library for future browsing and to show off to visiting parents and grandparents.

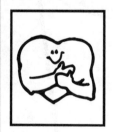

Values Education Experience

• Discuss the importance of honesty, in publishing and in our personal lives. If people find false statements in a magazine, will they want to continue buying it? If people find out that we don't tell the truth, will they listen to what we say?

Valentine's Day

February 14

Setting the Stage

• Display a picture of Cupid aiming his arrow at a giant heart that reads, "LOVE IS...." Then let students write their feelings about love on smaller hearts scattered around Cupid.

• Display hearts with *love* written in various languages with the caption: "Love means the same in any language."

Setting the Stage continued

- Cut a giant heart out of pink or red paper. Tell the class you will be "giving your heart away" all day. Throughout the day, cut off pieces of the paper heart, like a jigsaw puzzle, and write "love notes" of appreciation on them. Give them to students. Make sure that by the end of the day everyone has a note of appreciation. Explain that they are all a "part" of you and add much to your life! See heart pattern on page 104.

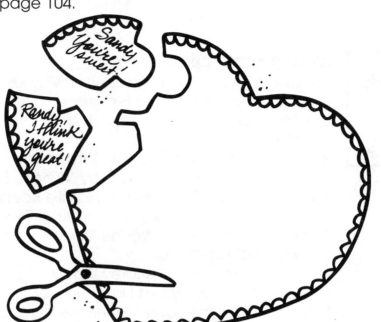

- Encourage those who want to bring valentine cards to bring one for every student so no one is left out.

- Construct a semantic web with facts your students know (or would like to know) about the human heart.

89

Historical Background

February 14th is Valentine's Day. No one knows when this tradition began, but some think it began with the Ancient Romans, named after a priest named Valentine. Esther Howland began the American tradition of sending cards when she started making lacy valentines and selling them in her father's shop.

Literary Exploration

Appolonia's Valentine by Katherine Milhous
Arthur's Valentine by Marc Brown
Bee My Valentine! by Miriam Cohen
Be My Valentine by M. J. Carr
Best Valentine Book by Patricia Whitehead
The Best Valentine in the World by Marjorie Sharmat
Bub: Or the Very Best Thing by Natalie Babbitt
A Circle Is Not a Valentine by H. Werner Zimmerman
Cranberry Valentine by Wende Devlin
Cupid by Babette Cole
Detective Valentine by Audrey Wood
Dinosaur Valentine by Liza Donnelly
Disney's Winnie the Pooh's Valentine by Bruce Talkington
Four Valentines in a Rainstorm by Felicia Bond
Freckles and Willie by Margery Cuyler
The Great Valentine's Day Balloon Race by Adrienne Adams
The Heart (Your Body series) by John Gaskin
"Heart" an excerpt from *I Wonder Why I Blink and Other Questions About My Body* by Brigid Avison
Hearts, Cupids and Red Roses by Edna Barth
I Love You, Mary Jane by Lorna Balian
It's Valentine's Day by Jack Prelutsky
Little Angels' Alphabet of Love by Joan Walsh Anglund
Little Love Story by Fernando Krahn
Little Mouse's Big Valentine by Thacher Hurd
The Little Prince by Antoine de Saint-Exupéry
Louanne Pig in the Mysterious Valentine by Nancy Carlson
Love Is a Special Way of Feeling by Joan Walsh Anglund
Love Is Walking Hand-in-Hand by Charles Schulz
Miss Flora McFlimsey's Valentine by Mariana
Monster Valentines by Joanna Cole
My Book of Funny Valentines by Margo Lundell
One Zillion Valentines by Frank Modell
Pleasant Fieldmouse's Valentine Trick by Jan Wahl
Saint Valentine by Robert Sabuda
Secret Valentine by Laura Damon
Secret Valentine by Catherine Stock
Somebody Loves You, Mr. Hatch by Eileen Spinelli
Sparky's Valentine Victory by Marilyn Walton

Literary Exploration continued

A Sweetheart for Valentine by Lorna Balian
Valentine by Carol Carrick
The Valentine Bears by Eve Bunting
The Valentine Cat by Clyde Bulla
A Valentine Fantasy by Carolyn Haywood, et al
A Valentine for Cousin Archie by Barbara Williams
Valentine for a Dragon by Shirley Rousseau Murphy
A Valentine for Fuzzboom by True Kelly
Valentine Foxes by Clyde Watson
Valentine Friends by Ann Schweninger
The Valentine Kittens by Stephanie St. Pierre
The Valentine Party by Pamela Bianco
Valentine's Day by Gail Gibbons
Valentine's Day by Miriam Nerlove
The Valentine Star by Patricia Reilly Giff
What Color Is Love? by Joan Walsh Anglund
Where Is Nicky's Valentine? by Harriet Ziefert
Will You Be My Valentine? by Steven Kroll

Language Experience

• Have students alphabetize their valentine cards by the names signed on them to reinforce alphabetizing.

• Let each student make a small valentine heart that can be pinned on the back of the student's dress or shirt. Each heart should contain a noun which another person has to try and identify by asking questions that can only be answered with a "yes" or "no." (As in "Twenty Questions.")

• Challenge students to brainstorm ways to show others that we love them.

Writing Experience

• Love is difficult to explain, but after discussing it, let students write about how it makes them feel to love someone.

• Students can list all the people who love and care about them, then all the people they love and care about. When they have exhausted their love lists, ask them to write about how it feels to be surrounded by so much love.

• Let students cut pictures of fruits and vegetables from used seed packets and catalogs. Challenge them to come up with Valentine puns to go with the pictures (Examples: If you CARROT all for me . . . or My heart BEETS for you! You and I make a great PEAR.)

• See reproducible for writing activities on page 105.

Math Experience

- Take advantage of the high interest today in the giving and receiving of valentines to have students help you write Valentine story problems to solve. (Example: Sarah has three kitten valentines, one robot valentine and four airplane valentines. How many does she have in all? If she gives two away, how many will she have left?)

- Let students cut out hearts of different sizes, then arrange them in order of size from smallest to largest.

⚠ Fill a jar with candy hearts. Let students estimate the number in the jar, writing it and their name on a piece of paper. Let students list the guesses from the smallest number to the greatest on the board. Later in the day, count the candy hearts together (practicing number sequence). Give the jar to the person with the closest estimate so he or she can share with the others.

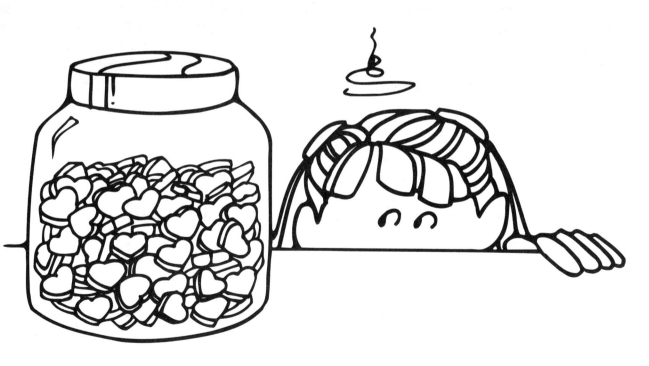

Math Experience continued

- Students can cut out heart shapes, then cut them down the center. On one heart half they write a math review problem and on the other half, the answer. Then they exchange the heart pieces with other student hearts. At your signal, they go around the room trying to match their hearts.

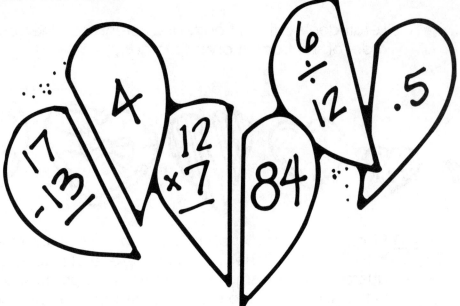

Science/Health Experience

- This is a great chance to study the heart and its functions. Try to borrow a plastic model of the human heart. Explain that the heart is a muscle that pumps blood through the arteries and veins throughout the body. We need food and water, exercise and fresh air to keep our bodies healthy. The heart is located in the center of our chest. The pumping takes place on the left, so you feel it beating on the left side of your chest. A student can place a toilet paper tube over another student's heart to listen for the beating. Have the listener say "beep" every time he or she hears it beating to illustrate that everyone's heart does not beat at the same rate. The beating is actually the closing valve allowing blood to pump in and out of the heart. If a local butcher has a cow heart you can use, show the size difference between a human heart and an animal heart. Each student can make a fist to show the approximate size of his or her own heart.

Science/Health Experience continued

• On the board draw a diagram of the human heart. Have students copy it labeling the parts and functions of each area of the heart.

• Explain how to keep the heart healthy through choosing not to smoke or drink alcohol, eating healthy foods low in fat and getting adequate rest and exercise. Check out a heart education kit from your local American Heart Association (especially for primary grades).

Music/Dramatic Experience

• Teach students how to say "I love you" in another language: Yo te amo (Spanish); Lo to amo (Italian); Je t'aime (French); Ich liebe dich (German); Ai shite imasu (Japanese)!

Physical/Sensory Experience

• Place a pail of water and red food coloring in a sink area to illustrate with a syringe or a turkey baster how blood is pulled in and pumped out of our hearts. Let students take turns "pulling the liquid in and pumping it out" like the human heart functions.

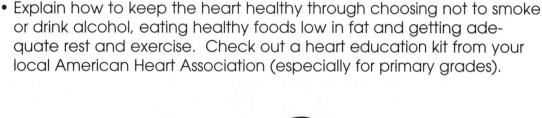

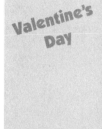

Physical/Sensory Experience continued

- Illustrate how to check for the pulse. Point out that the places to check for a pulse (wrist or neck) are close to main arteries where we can actually feel the blood traveling or pumping through the circulatory system. Have students run in place, then check their pulse again noting the change in rapidity after exercise. Explain that the heart is a muscle and, like any other muscle, it will weaken with neglect. It needs exercise to maintain its strength and vitality. Do some simple calisthenics such as jumping jacks and jumping rope together! Then have students check their pulse again.

- Play Musical Valentine Hearts! Students stand behind chairs with valentine cards on the desks. One desk will not have a valentine. When the music starts, they begin walking around the desks until the music stops. Then they must sit quickly in the nearest chair. Whoever sits in the chair with no valentine on the desk is out. Remove a valentine card from an arbitrary desk after each go-around. Finally the one person left gets to pass out his or her valentines to everyone.

Physical/Sensory Experience continued

• Divide students into teams. Give everyone a drinking straw. The first player in each line is given a tissue paper heart. The players must inhale and keep the tissue hearts sucked onto the end of their straws as they pass them along to the next players in line. No hands allowed! The first team that finishes wins.

Valentine's Day

Valentine's Day

• Have students cut valentine hearts in half at odd angles (like puzzle pieces). They place one of the halves in a common pile with everyone else's halves. One at a time, each student grabs someone else's half heart and sits down. At your signal, they hurry to match their puzzle pieces. When students complete their heart puzzles, they hurry and sit down. The first one done is the King or Queen of Hearts for the day.

Valentine's Day

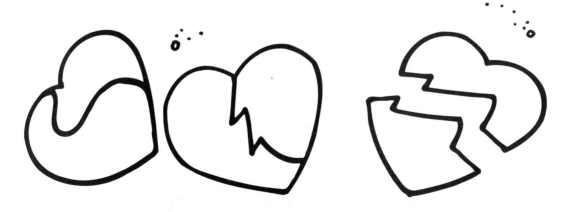

Valentine's Day

Physical/Sensory Experience

- At your signal, each student tears a piece of red paper into a heart shape behind his or her back. When time is up and another signal is given, award candy hearts for the most creative, largest or most symmetrical hearts.

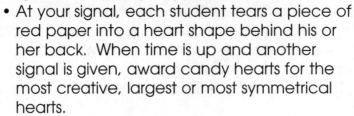

- Set up a small-mouthed jar or bottle. Challenge students to throw candy hearts into the mouth of the jar. Whoever gets the most candy hearts in is the winner.

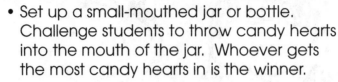

- Have a puzzle relay. Each team leader is given a sandwich bag with heart puzzle pieces in it. Players put the puzzle together as they pass it along each one adding a piece. When the last person on a team has finished the puzzle, that team wins! See pattern on page 106.

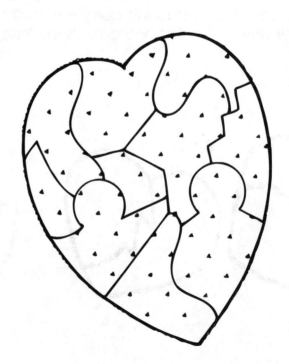

Physical/Sensory Experience continued

• Students can have fun practicing their manual dexterity with this coordination game. Divide them into teams. The first player on each team is handed a pair of chopsticks or toothpicks. They pick up valentine heart candies with them and transport them over to a given area, they run back and place the chopsticks or toothpicks on a table for the next person to use. To make it even more of a challenge, let players use only one hand!

• Blindfold one student at a time and play Pin Cupid's Arrow on the Heart (like Pin the Tail on the Donkey). See patterns on page 107.

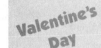

• Play Drop the Handkerchief, but substitute a red beanbag for the handkerchief.

Valentine's
Day

Valentine's
Day

Valentine's
Day

Arts/Crafts Experience

• Let students make valentine holders by cutting out two large matching hearts, folding the top heart down about two inches and stapling them together. Students can write their names in their best handwriting on the scalloped edge. They can then decorate them by outlining the name in glitter. When the glue and glitter is dry, hang students' paper hearts on the edge of their desks so other students can put valentines in them when time permits.

• Students can decorate valentine mailboxes. Provide them with empty tissue boxes, pink and red construction paper, lacy hearts or doilies, wrapping paper, ribbon, glitter and glue. Encourage them to let their imaginations run wild!

Arts/Crafts Experience continued

- Students can make heart sachets by sewing two red or pink felt hearts together, leaving an opening in which to stuff a cotton ball that has been scented with perfume. Then the opening can be sewn shut.

- Students can lace ribbon or yarn through a hole-punched heart shape to practice eye-hand coordination.

- Students will enjoy making "stained-glass" hearts. They shave red, pink and white crayons onto wax paper, then lay another piece of wax paper on top of the crayon shavings. An adult can run a slightly warm iron over the wax paper. The shavings will melt into a beautiful design which can be framed by the outline of a heart.

- Let students make tissue paper hearts by filling a heart shape with colored tissue paper squares dipped in glue. Fit tissue paper squares around the eraser end of a pencil. Dip into a small amount of glue and press into place on the paper heart. Remove pencil gently, leaving tissue paper in place.

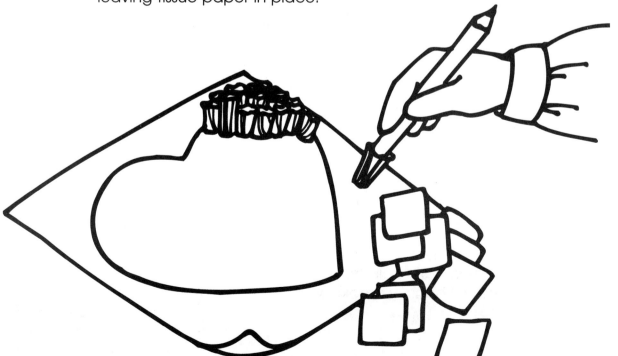

Arts/Crafts Experience continued

- A pear shape cut out of red paper can become a valentine lovebird. Add two red heart-shaped wings folded in half, a yellow beak and two legs.

- Cut heart shapes from sponges and let students sponge paint prints to decorate homemade valentine cards.

- Provide students with black construction paper and craft sticks for the frame on an old-time chalkboard slate. They glue the craft sticks around the construction paper, then write with white chalk on the black center: *2 Sweet 2 Bee 4 Gotten* like a math equation. Add an addition sign and a line under the twos. A pink or red heart can be added in a corner to add a little color.

Extension Activities

⚠ Make valentine cupcakes together. Before putting the cupcake batter in the cupcake liners to bake, put a marble between the edge of the liner and cupcake pan. As you pour the batter, make sure the cupcake batter goes around the marble to create a heart shape. After the cupcakes cool, students can decorate them with pink frosting (white frosting with red food coloring). Serve cupcakes with red or pink punch and red licorice sticks with the ends cut so they can be used as a straw!

⚠ Students will enjoy eating "Sweetheart Salad." Mix a can of cherry pie filling, a can of pineapple tidbits and a cup of miniature marshmallows with a couple of sliced bananas and chill!

⚠ Make valentine-shaped pancakes using metal heart-shaped cookie cutters. With help from parents, you and your class can start the day with a "heart"y breakfast!

Extension Activities continued

⚠ Make valentine cookies and have students decorate them to take to children in a nearby hospital to brighten their day.

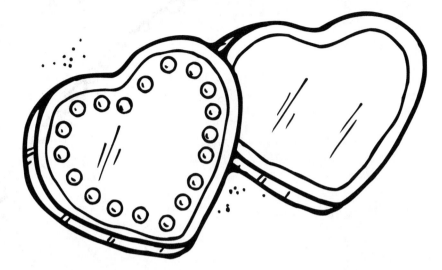

• Put several items including some valentine objects (heart shaped candle, valentine card, candy, flower) on a tray. Have students look at it and try to remember everything on the tray. Then they close their eyes while you remove an object. Can they identify what was removed? Mix up the objects and keep playing.

⚠ "Sweetheart" biscuits are made by shaping refrigerator biscuit dough into heart shapes. Roll them in butter and cinnamon sugar and bake according to the package instructions. Your students will enjoy them for a snack.

Values Education Experience

• Discuss some practical ways to show love to others.

Follow-Up/Homework Idea

• Challenge students to express their love to their families today (and every day).

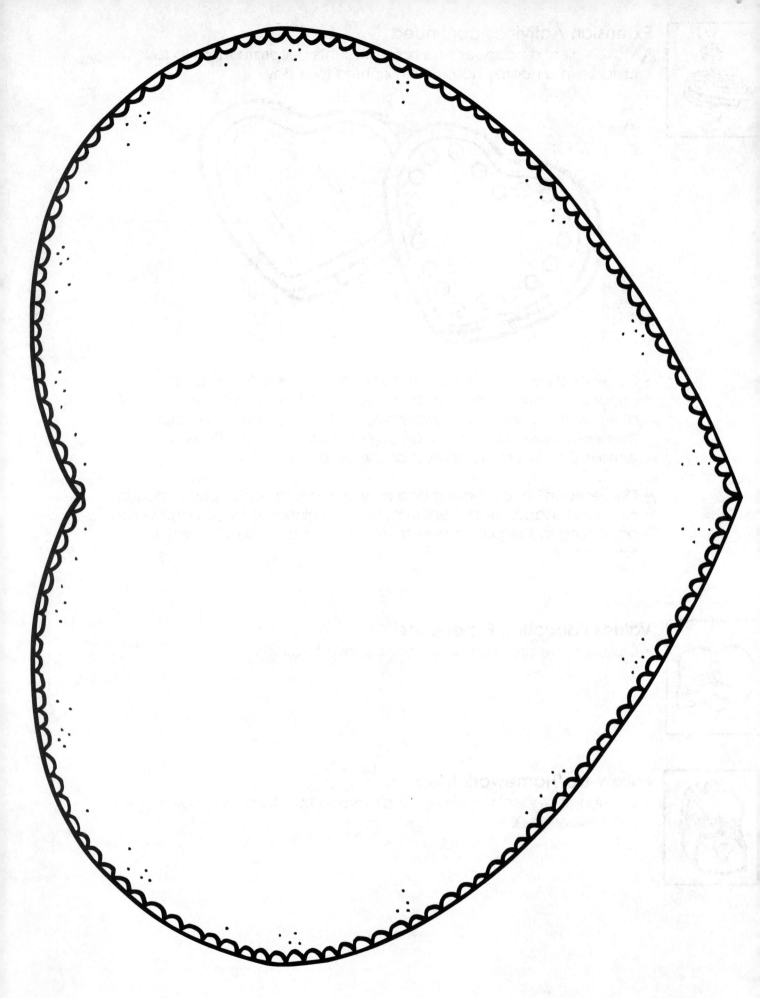

104

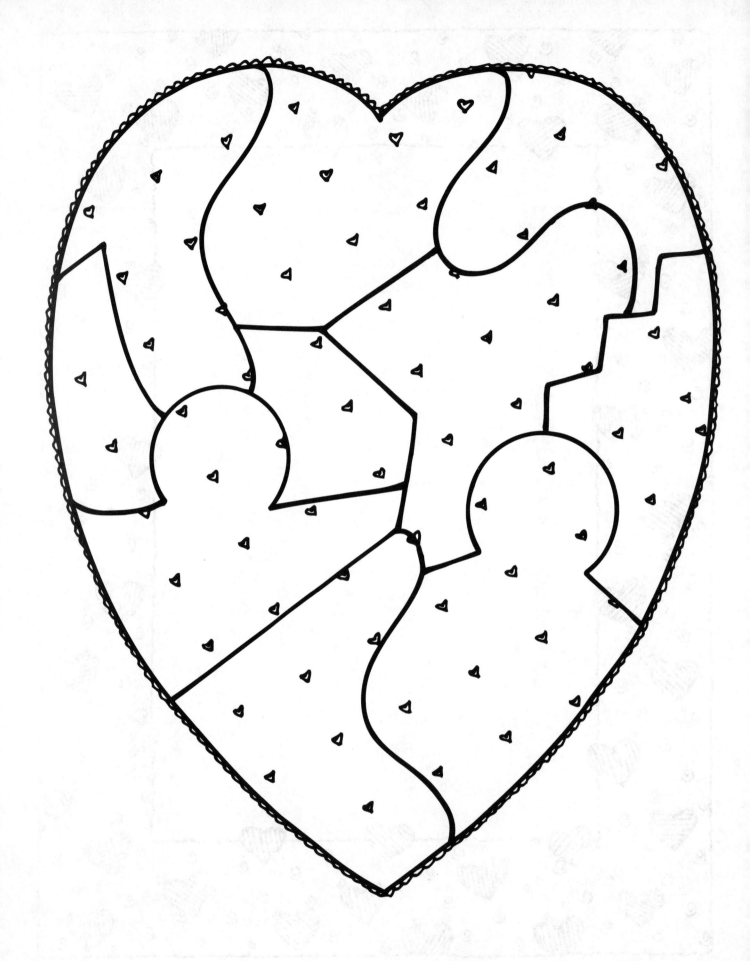

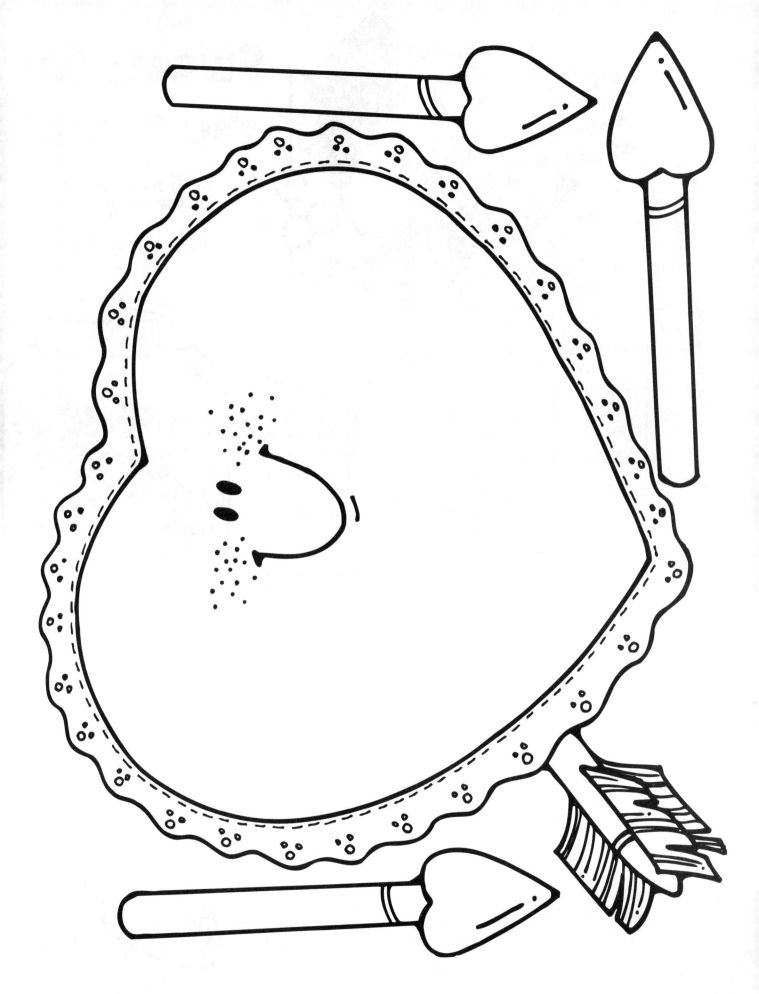

Sweets for the Sweet Day

February 15

Setting the Stage

• Begin this delicious day by displaying a large jar of "sweets." Encourage acts of kindness (being "sweet") by dropping another "sweet" in the jar each time you see students being kind. Share the contents of the jar whenever you feel it's a good time. (Save money by buying leftover valentine candy).

• Leave candy bar wrappers around the room to get students' attention.

• Construct a semantic map or web with facts your students already know about candy. Ask them to list what else they would like to learn about candy today.

Historical Background

Milton Hershey was born in 1857 and grew up to build the world's largest chocolate factory in Hershey, Pennsylvania. Chocolate is very popular, but there are also many other kinds of candies popular in America. Americans definitely have a "sweet tooth."

Literary Exploration

The Candy Corn Contest by Patricia Reilly Giff
Charlie and the Chocolate Factory by Roald Dahl
The Chocolate Cow by Lilian Obligado
Chocolate Fever by Robert K. Smith
A Chocolate Moose for Dinner by Fred Gwynne
Chocolate Mud Cake by Harriet Ziefert
The Chocolate Rabbit by Maria Claret
The Chocolate Touch by Patrick Skene Catling
The Chocolate Wedding by Posy Simmonds
Cocoa Beans and Daisies: How Swiss Chocolate
   Is Made by Pascale Allamand
From Cacao Bean to Chocolate by Ali Mitgutsch
Gumboot's Chocolatey Day by Mick Inkpen
Max's Chocolate Chicken by Rosemary Wells
The Sweet Touch by Lorna Balian

Language Experience

• After reading *A Chocolate Moose for Dinner* by Fred Gwynne, introduce or review figures of speech. Another great book by the same author (along the same lines) is *The King Who Rained.*

• Make a large candy gram for your school principal, secretary or librarian. Write it on poster board and use mini candy bars for some of the words. Let students be creative about how they use candy in the message.

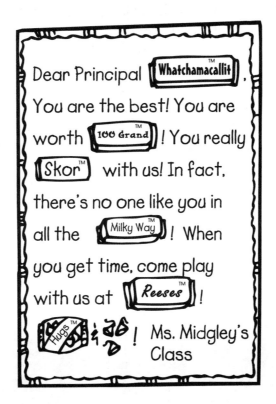

Dear Principal Whatchamacallit™,
You are the best! You are
worth 100 Grand™! You really
Skor™ with us! In fact,
there's no one like you in
all the Milky Way™! When
you get time, come play
with us at Reeses™!
Hugs™ ♥ ! Ms. Midgley's
Class

Language Experience continued

- Display candy bars and let students practice alphabetizing the candy bar names.

- Let students survey classmates about their favorite kinds of candy bars, then put the information on a class graph.

- Let students suggest new names for their favorite candies. The names should say something about the shape, size, appearance or taste of the candies.

- Brainstorm descriptive or sensory imagery after having a taste test of some of your favorite sweets.

Writing Experience

- Hershey's candy bar was named after him. What kind of food would your students like to have named after them? Have them put their ideas down on paper.

- Let students imagine that they looked out the window and it started raining candy! Let them write a story about what happened.

- Students can write to the Hershey Corporation and ask for a booklet about the history of chocolate. They can also send their questions to:

      Hershey Foods Corporation
      Public Relations Department
      P.O. Box 814
      Hershey, PA 17033

- Divide students into cooperative groups. Have each group read the ingredients on candy bar wrappers and write what they think the ingredients are. (Examples: sodium stearoyl lactylate, mono-and diglycerides, dextrose or TBHQ.)

Writing Experience

⚠ Give each student a round peppermint candy and a paper plate. Let students examine the peppermint, visually, smell it, feel its surface and then pop it in their mouths. Have them think of words that describe that peppermint sensation (cool, tingly, colorful, striped, smooth). In the center of the paper plate, they write descriptive words or phrases. Then they can paint the edges of the plate red and white to resemble the peppermint. Display them on your classroom walls.

Tiny
Noisy Wrapper
Tasty
Minty
Crunchy
Red & White
Delicious
Round
Hard

• See reproducible for various writing assignments on page 116.

Math Experience

- Americans eat almost six million pounds of chocolate a day! Have students estimate about how much that would be for the average person each day. (First, students will need to find out the current population in America.)

- Review perimeter and area concepts with students by measuring candy bars. Have students measure different kinds of candy bars in inches, centimeters and grams. If you have access to scales, let them also measure weight to the nearest gram.

⚠ Let students guess the number of candies in a jar. Award the candy to the one whose guess is the closest.

⚠ Have fun with candy graphing! Supply students with jellybeans and other small colored candies. Create class or individual bar graphs, line graphs or pictographs illustrating the distribution of colors. Before any graphing is done, give students time to estimate their individual candies and then to check for the actual amount. Let them classify their candy by colors and the amount of each color. Then they can begin graphing, tallying the amount of each color. Have them make pictures or patterns with alternating colors of candy. They can duplicate a given pattern and create their own patterns. What a fun way to sweeten up math!

Science/Health Experience

- Learn about the science of chocolate! Research how chocolate originates from the cacao seed which grows into a cacao tree, producing pods that contain 30 or 40 bitter-tasting beans. These beans are sent to factories where they are roasted and cracked opened to remove the center. The center of the bean is crushed into a liquor which, when added with other ingredients, is used to make chocolate products.

- Which kinds of candies float, sink or dissolve when put in water? Let students experiment.

Social Studies Experience

• Discuss what kinds of manners are "sweet" and which are "semi-sweet" (not so sweet).

Music/Dramatic Experience

• Divide students into groups and give each a different kind of candy. Challenge them to come up with new slogans, jingles or advertisements to increase sales.

Arts/Crafts Experience

• Unwrap several types of candy and let students examine the packaging and the design. Let them create their own candy wrapper designs. Provide rulers, aluminum foil, markers, paper, scissors and glue. They should include important details on the wrappers (ingredients, weight, description, etc.).

Arts/Crafts Experience continued

• Let students create a Hansel and Gretel house! Get an empty, refrigerator box from an appliance store. Attach butcher paper to the sides, then the students go crazy decorating the "house" with treats every child loves.

Extension Activities

• Provide the board game Candy Land™ for students to play if they get finished with their class work early.

⚠ Write a note of praise or encouragement on a tiny slip of paper and tape it to a Hershey's Kiss™ for each student. Leave them on students' desks.

⚠ Melt semi-sweet chocolate chips and pour them into ice cube trays. Stick a craft stick in each one and freeze for a few minutes until hardened. Your students will enjoy the treats!

114

Extension Activities continued

⚠ Make homemade candy by dipping braided pretzels into melted chocolate. Melt chocolate chips illustrating for students how chocolate goes from solid to liquid, then back again to solid form in candy as it cools on the pretzels.

• Let students make candy leis. Buy bulk candy at a discount store. You'll also need plastic wrap and colorful yarn. Have students measure and cut about two feet of plastic wrap on a smooth, flat surface. They arrange pieces of candy down the length of it leaving spaces between each piece. Then they wrap the ends of the plastic wrap around the candies. They cut yarn pieces and tie them in bows between the candies. They tie both ends of the lei together and have a candy lei. Aloha!

• If there is a candy factory near your school, take your class on a field trip and have them make observational drawings.

• Have a candy scavenger hunt. Write directions on candy wrappers and leave them all around the school. Students can follow the directions to the candy.

116

Television News Day

February 16

Setting the Stage

• Dress like a television news reporter (microphone in hand) and greet your students by "reporting" what they are going to learn about television news today!

• Construct a semantic map with facts your students already know about television news. Then invite them to list questions they have about television news reports to help you structure your activities today.

Historical Background

The first television news broadcast was presented on this day in 1948.

Literary Exploration

A Day in the Life of a Television News Reporter by William Jaspersohn

Language Experience

- Create a Venn diagram with the similarities and differences between television news and radio news broadcasts.

- Let your student browse through the current news of the day and make notes.

Writing Experience

- After students research world and local news, have them write the information in a television broadcast "script." Divide students into cooperative groups, letting each person be responsible for reporting one aspect of the news (world news, local news, weather, sports, etc.) to the rest of the class or school.

Social Studies Experience

- Let students watch a TV news broadcast to see how it is put together. Discuss all the people needed behind and in front of the cameras: reporters, photographers, camera men, set designers, on-air anchors, etc.

Music/Dramatic Experience

- Have students present their group broadcasts "on air" (videotape). Each group can be called a different news station such as "Channel 2 News." Encourage students to use newsroom "lingo" and phrases such as, "And now back to you, Jane!"

Arts/Crafts Experience

• Let students create or paint newsroom "backdrops" of scenery for their news presentations.

Extension Activities

• After the news broadcasts have been videotaped, play them back for students to see them on the television through the use of a videotape and VCR.

• Invite a local newscaster to come and share information about his or her work.

• If you live close enough, take a field trip to a local newsroom and watch the pros in action!

Values Education Experience

• Discuss what *responsible journalism* means. Why do news reporters need to be "unbiased"?

Follow-Up/Homework Idea

• Encourage students to watch the television news at home with their parents this evening.

Black History Day

February 17

Setting the Stage

- Display pictures and books of famous African Americans such as James Weldon Johnson; Rebecca Cole; Martin Luther King, Jr.; Marian Anderson; Langston Hughes; Harriet Tubman; Michael Jordan; Colin Powell; Bill Cosby; etc. Choose people from a variety of occupations.

- Construct a semantic web with facts your students already know (or would like to know) about what African Americans have contributed to this nation.

Historical Background

Actually, the whole month of February is National Black History month. It has been set aside as a time to recognize achievements and contributions by African Americans. Begun in 1926 as a one-week observance, it was changed to the whole month of February in 1976.

Literary Exploration

Afro-Bets Book of Black Heroes from A to Z by Wade Hudson and Valerie Wilson Wesley
Booker T. Washington by Shirley Graham
Don't You Turn Back: Poems by Langston Hughes
Eight Black American Inventors by Robert Hayden
The Sweet and Sour Animal Book by Langston Hughes

Language Experience

• Let students research their favorite African Americans. Then they can pretend to be those people as classmates interview them about their lives and accomplishments.

Social Studies Experience

• Study influential African Americans throughout history (Frederick Douglass, Phyllis Wheatley, Rosa Parks, Booker T. Washington, etc.) Also talk about African American athletes that have contributed so much to our sports culture (Jackie Robinson, Hank Aaron, Muhammad Ali, Michael Jordan).

Music/Dramatic Experience

• One famous African American was Marian Anderson, the first African American to sing with the Metropolitan Opera of New York in 1955. She became a delegate to the United Nations and received a Congressional Gold Medal in 1978. Check out a tape of her singing from the public library and play it for your students. Then for contrast, play some jazz by famous trumpeter Louis Armstrong or Dizzy Gillespie.

Physical/Sensory Experience

• Play some music by popular African American musicians (Chuck Berry, the Platters or other rock-and-roll stars) and let students dance.

Arts/Crafts Experience

• Let students research their favorite African Americans and paint portraits of them. Display the labeled portraits on a bulletin board with the caption: "Our Salute to African Americans."

Extension Activities

• Invite two or three African Americans from the community (from various occupations) to visit your class to talk about the challenges of being black in America. Let students ask them questions.

Values Education Experience

• Discuss prejudice. Why is it wrong to judge people by things such as skin color, intelligence, etc.? Talk about the importance of accepting others as we would like to be accepted.

Follow-Up/Homework Idea

• Challenge students to show kindness to everyone they meet, no matter what their color of skin, size, age or way of dressing or talking.

Brotherhood/ Sisterhood Day

February 18

Setting the Stage

• Have students trace their hands on paper. Display the handprints around a map of the world on a bulletin board with the caption: "Let's Join Hands and Work Together!"

• Construct a semantic web with the words your students think of when they hear the words *brotherhood* and *sisterhood*. List questions they have about the words to help you plan the day's activities.

Historical Background

Brotherhood/Sisterhood Week is the third full week of February. It is a time to fight bigotry and racism in America and to promote under-standing and respect among all races, religions and cultures

Literary Exploration

The Big Book for Peace by Ann Durell and Marilyn Sachs
The Butter Battle Book by Dr. Suess
Fighting Words by Eve Merriam
Five Minutes' Peace by Jill Murphy
The Flame of Peace by Deborah Lattimore
The Great Peace March by Holly Near
How to Turn War into Peace by Louise Armstrong
Julius, the Baby of the World by Kevin Henkes
The Peace and Quiet Diner by Gregory Maguire
Peace at Last by Jill Murphy
Peace Begins with You by Katherine Scholes
Peace Crane by Sheila Hamanaka
Peace on the Playground by Eileen Lucas
People of Peace by Rose Blue
Ralph Bunche, Champion of Peace by Jean Cornell
The Story of Ferdinand by Munro Leaf
Tanya and the Green-Eyed Monster by Jonathan Sherwood, et al

Writing Experience

- Ask students to write about what they think people can do to show respect for one another and live at peace with everyone.

- Have students write poems about the importance of accepting other people as they are.

- See reproducible for writing activities on page 128.

Brotherhood Sisterhood

Brotherhood Sisterhood

Brotherhood Sisterhood

Math Experience

• Play Around the World Math! One student stands behind another student sitting at a desk. When you call out a math problem, both students try to say the answer as fast as they can. Whoever says the correct answer first gets to move to the next desk. The goal is for each student to go around the "world" or as many desks as possible before having to sit down.

Social Studies Experience

• Have students research wars in history. How many were caused by prejudice or intolerance?

• Invite interested students to research influential people throughout history who have been advocates of peace (Gandhi; Martin Luther King, Jr.; etc.), then share the information with the class.

Music/Dramatic Experience

• Sing the song, "I'd Like to Teach the World to Sing."

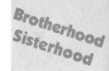

• Have students role-play conflict situations they might encounter on the playground or in the classroom. How can they be peacemakers? (Example: An older student tries to take away your lunch. What choices can you make?)

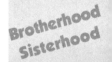

Physical/Sensory Experience

- Join hands for peace to play a game of Red Rover.

- Encourage students to think of ways they are alike instead of ways they are different. Every time they observe a way they are like a classmate, they can "high-five" that person.

Red Rover, Red Rover, send Charlie right over !!!

Arts/Crafts Experience

- Let students illustrate a classroom mural showing people of many kinds and races cooperating and getting along.

- Create a world flag quilt. Let students use rectangles of muslin or other fabric and fabric markers to make flags from around the world. They can be stitched together to form a classroom quilt.

Arts/Crafts Experience continued

• Students can make paper peace symbols (circles with an upside-down looking "Y" and a line down the middle). In each section of the symbol, they can draw a way to create a more peaceful world. You may want to share "peacemaking" ideas before they draw. See reproducible on page 129.

Name: _____

Extension Activities

⚠ Give each student a small bag of multicolored candies as a reminder that people may be many different sizes, shapes and colors, but we're basically all the same, so we should be "sweet" to everyone!

Values Education Experience

• Discuss the importance of respecting other people. How do we treat people we respect?

Follow-Up/Homework Idea

• Challenge students to show respect and acceptance to their parents, bus drivers, teachers and fellow students.

Brotherhood
Sisterhood

Brotherhood
Sisterhood

Brotherhood
Sisterhood

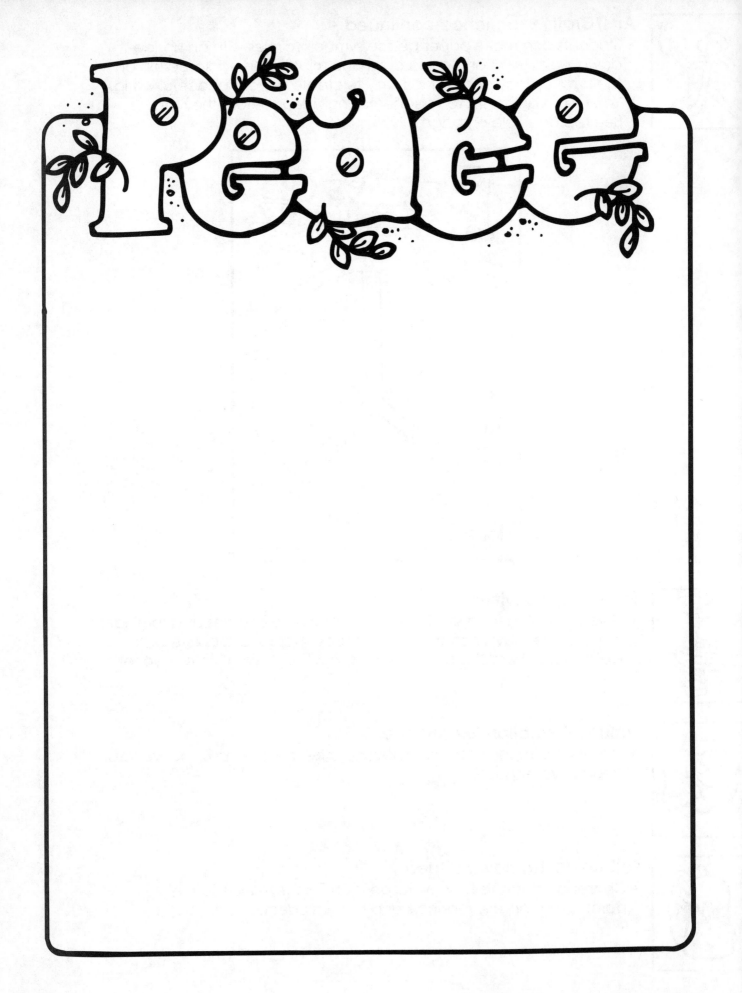

Name: _____

Copernicus' Birthday

February 19

Setting the Stage

• Take an intergalactic trip out of this world today with your studies of the solar system! Display space pictures and related literature to gather excitement in today's activities.

• Construct a semantic map or web with the facts your students already know (or want to know) about astronomy.

130

Historical Background

Nicholaus Copernicus, the Polish astronomer, was born on this day in 1473. He discovered that the sun, not the Earth, is the center of the solar system.

Literary Exploration

Alistair in Outer Space by Marilyn Sadler
Astronomy Today by Dinah L. Moche
Beyond the Milky Way by Cecile Schoberle
A Day in Space by Suzanne Lord
Exploring the Solar System by Peter Seymour
Fun Facts About the Solar System by William Cromie
Giant Book of Things in Space by George Zaffo
Insects from Outer Space by Frank Asch
It Came from Outer Space by Tony Bradman
The Magic School Bus Lost in the Solar System by Joanna Cole
Miss Pickerell Goes to Mars by Ellen MacGregor
Mr. Munday and the Space Creatures by Bonnie Pryor
My First Book About Space by Dinah L. Moche
My First Book of Space by Robert A. Bell
My Place in Space by Robin and Sally Hirst
Our Solar System by Seymour Simon
The Planets by Gail Gibbons
Planets by Kim Jackson
The Planets in Our Solar System by Franklyn Branley
Space by James Seevers
Space Case by Edward Marshall
Space Rock by Jon Buller and Susan Schade
Space Science Projects for Young Scientists by David W. McKay
Space Spinners by Suse MacDonald
Sun, Stars and Planets by McKissack
The Sun, Stars and Planets by Tom Stacy, et al
The Sun, Our Nearest Star by Franklyn M. Branley
The Third Planet: Exploring the Earth from Space by Sally Ride and Tam O'Shaughnessy
Trouble in Space by Rose Greydanus
What's Out There?: A Book About Space by Lynn Wilson

Language Experience

- Have students name the planets in our solar system, then alphabetize them.

- Introduce students to the literary genre of science fiction.

Writing Experience

- Have students imagine themselves looking through a telescope late at night and discovering an entirely new planet! What will they do first? How will they describe their planet to the media? Does this new planet show life? What will they name it? How will the discovery of this new planet affect them and others? They should write down their observations and feelings. See reproducible on page 137.

132

Math Experience

• Can we measure the distance between planets in the solar system? Not exactly, but students can measure on a smaller scale on your own school blacktop. Divide them into cooperative groups, each assuming responsibility for a different task. The first group draws a large sun with yellow chalk. Then they measure 1$\frac{3}{4}$" (with a yardstick) from the sun. The next group draws and labels Mercury at that point, then measures a distance of 3$\frac{1}{4}$" for the next group. The third group draws and labels Venus at that spot, then measures 4$\frac{3}{4}$" where the next group will draw and label Earth, then measure 7" for Mars and so on.

• The final drawing should reflect these distances:

Mercury—1$\frac{3}{4}$" from the sun
Venus—3$\frac{1}{4}$" from the sun
Earth—4$\frac{3}{4}$" from the sun
Mars—7" from the sun
Jupiter—2' $\frac{1}{4}$" from the sun
Saturn—3' 8$\frac{1}{4}$" from the sun
Uranus—7' 5" from the sun
Neptune—11' 7$\frac{1}{2}$" from the sun
Pluto—15' 3" from the sun
One inch represents about 20 million miles!

Copernicus

Copernicus

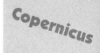

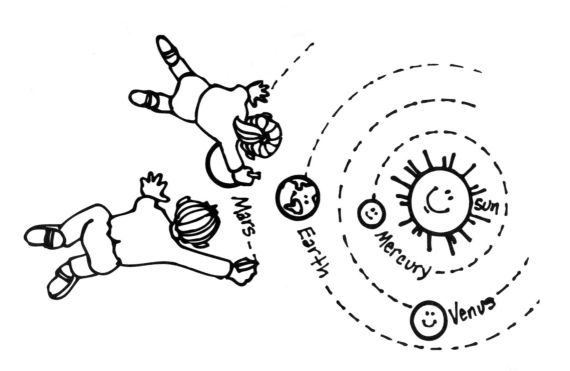

Copernicus

Math Experience continued

⚠ Review subtraction skills by giving students cereal shapes to represent "space ships" for subtraction manipulatives. (Example: 10 space ships soared into the solar system, but only 3 returned. How many were lost in a black hole? (The black hole can be students' mouths.)

Science/Health Experience

• Begin a science unit on the solar system today.

• Have students research to discover the importance of the Earth's location in space for our well being. (Closer to the sun and we'd burn up; farther away and we'd freeze.)

• Encourage interested students to research specific planets or astronomers (Galileo, Halley, Newton), then share their findings with the rest of the class.

• Have students work together on a mural of the solar system, labeling planets and including interesting facts about space.

Social Studies Experience

• Have students investigate the history of astronomy. Write significant discoveries about our solar system on a time line.

Physical/Sensory Experience

• Set up a trash can to be a Black Hole in space. Students make paper rocket ships and fly them from a distance, trying to get them into the Black Hole.

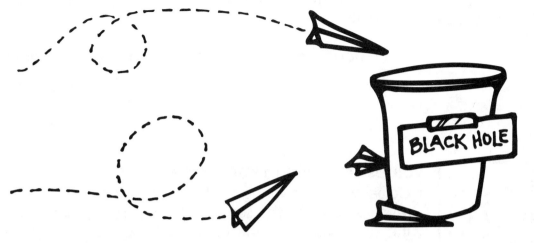

• Play Rings Around Saturn. Students attempt to toss rubber canning jar rings around large, round sticker shapes on the floor.

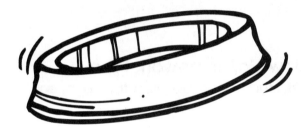

Arts/Crafts Experience

• Create a model of the solar system with various sizes of Styrofoam™ balls hung on a coat hanger.

• Students can draw pictures of the planets in space, pressing heavily with crayons, then washing a layer of black watercolor over the picture.

Extension Activities

⚠ Serve miniature Milky Way™ candy bars or make "Milky Way Milk Shakes" by blending ice cream and a favorite topping in a blender.

• Invite an astronomer to your class to show slides and talk about his or her work.

• Visit a nearby planetarium for an interesting and informative field trip.

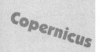

Values Education Experience

• Copernicus was willing to stand alone in his belief that the Earth revolved around the sun though popular opinion disagreed (believing the Earth was the center of everything). Discuss the tenacity and strength he needed to stick to his beliefs when challenged. What can we learn from Copernicus' example?

Follow-Up/Homework Idea

• Ask students to observe the night sky tonight with or without a telescope.

136

John Glenn Day

February 20

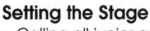

Setting the Stage

- Calling all junior astronauts! Display space paraphernalia (pictures of astronauts in space, related books, toy rocket ships) to get students excited about today's emphasis. Dress up like an astronaut, wearing a sweat suit or jumpsuit, a big belt and a motorcycle helmet. Add official-looking pins and buttons for authenticity!

- Begin an incentive program with a space shuttle with each student's name on it on a bulletin board. Choose a goal you want to work on with each student (math facts, penmanship, behavior, punctuality, etc.). Explain that each student's goal is to advance from the Earth to other planets. Each time a student makes progress in a given area, he or she can move the space shuttle. See pattern on page 144.

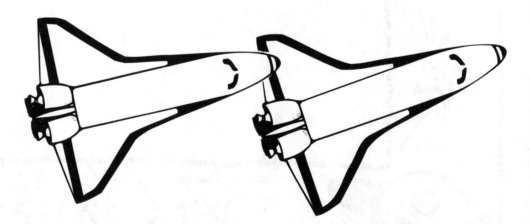

- Construct a semantic web with facts your students already know (or would like to know) about astronauts to help structure your day.

Historical Background

John Glenn made history on this day in 1962 by being the first American astronaut to orbit Earth!

Literary Exploration

A Is for Astronaut by Sian Tucker
A Day in Space by Suzanne Lord
The Giant Book of Things in Space by George Zaffo
I Can Be an Astronaut by June Behrens
I Want to Be an Astronaut by Byron Barton
I Want to Be a Space Pilot by Carla Greene
John Glenn: Astronaut and Senator by Michael Cole
John Glenn: Space Pioneer by Ann Angel
My Place in Space by Robin and Sally Hirst
Space Travelers by Margaret Wild
Space Vehicles by Anne Rockwell and David Brion
Trouble in Space by Rose Greydanus

John Glenn

Language Experience

• Have students brainstorm as many words as they can think of that rhyme with *space*.

John Glenn

Writing Experience

• Have students pretend to become astronauts. They should write letters of application explaining why they should be chosen for the next space shuttle flight.

• Let students imagine they are astronauts writing letters home. Is flying in space what they imagined before takeoff? What is the food like? How do they sleep? What supplies are on board? What do they do for entertainment? What message do they have for their families? Let them write all about their experiences.

John Glenn

Writing Experience

- Students can ask for more information about astronauts by writing to:
McDonnell Douglas
Box 516
St. Louis, MO 63166

- See reproducible for writing activities on page 145.

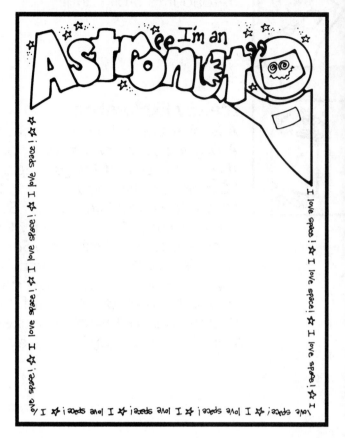

Science/Health Experience

- Experiment to discover how a space rocket gets off the ground! Thread a 12-foot piece of string through a drinking straw. Tie each end onto the back of a chair and move them apart until the string becomes taut. Put the straw at one end of the string. Blow up a balloon and pinch it closed (not tied). While holding the balloon closed, stick a piece of tape across the straw and onto the balloon. Keep the balloon opening in the opposite direction it will be heading. Release the balloon and the "thrust" will push the straw along the string. Explain that a rocket produces its own thrust so it can overcome the effects of the Earth's gravity.

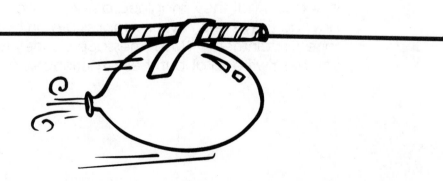

Social Studies Experience

- Have students research the life of John Glenn. Most students may not know of his other accomplishments. He was a pilot in both World War II and the Korean War. He broke the sound barrier during a $3\frac{1}{2}$-hour flight from New York to Los Angeles. After he left the space program, he became a senator from Ohio. Years later he became the oldest astronaut to fly in space at age 77.

- Study the history of space travel and other astronauts who have made significant contributions to the space program.

Music/Dramatic Experience

- Let students role-play being astronauts in space! Prepare for "liftoff," check instruments, securing an orbit or plotting a course. Check with "Mission Control." Walk weightless (in slow motion), etc. Let the students' creativity guide them!

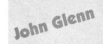

Physical/Sensory Experience

- Becoming an astronaut means undergoing rigorous training. Astronauts must be in excellent physical shape. Encourage students to get physically fit by exercising together.

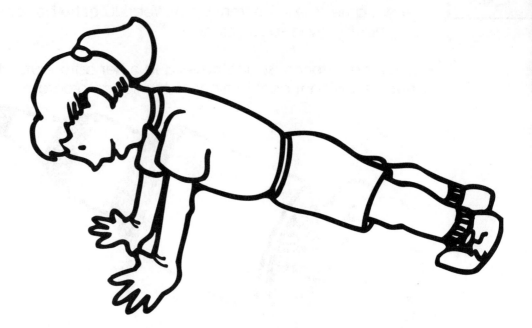

- Blindfold one student at a time and play Pin the Space Shuttle on the Moon (like Pin the Tail on the Donkey).

Arts/Crafts Experience

- Students can make space suits with large grocery bags for space helmets. Turn them upside down and cut out a rectangular viewing window. Pipe cleaners can be added for radio communications antenna on top of the helmet. An inverted carton can serve as the astronaut suit. Cut neck and armholes and hang over the shoulders. Two paper towel tubes or egg cartons can serve as oxygen tanks on the back panel of the suit. Ready for blastoff!

142

Arts/Crafts Experience continued

- Have students work together to make a Flip-Top Space Ship! Outline the space ship on a refrigerator box. Some students can work on the exterior of the ship while others work on the interior. Cut a space ship window and hang stars in front of it so when students are inside, they can look out into "space." Add a flashlight and books and game about space. Students who receive a "flight pass" from you can board the ship as time permits to read and contemplate space.

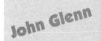

Extension Activities

⚠ Serve Tang™ (juice of astronauts), dried fruit and energy bars (or granola bars) just like the astronauts eat! And everyone loves miniature Mars™ candy bars.

Follow-Up/Homework Idea

- Encourage students to "sleep over" in another room of the house tonight and pretend they are sleeping in space.

John Glenn

John Glenn

John Glenn

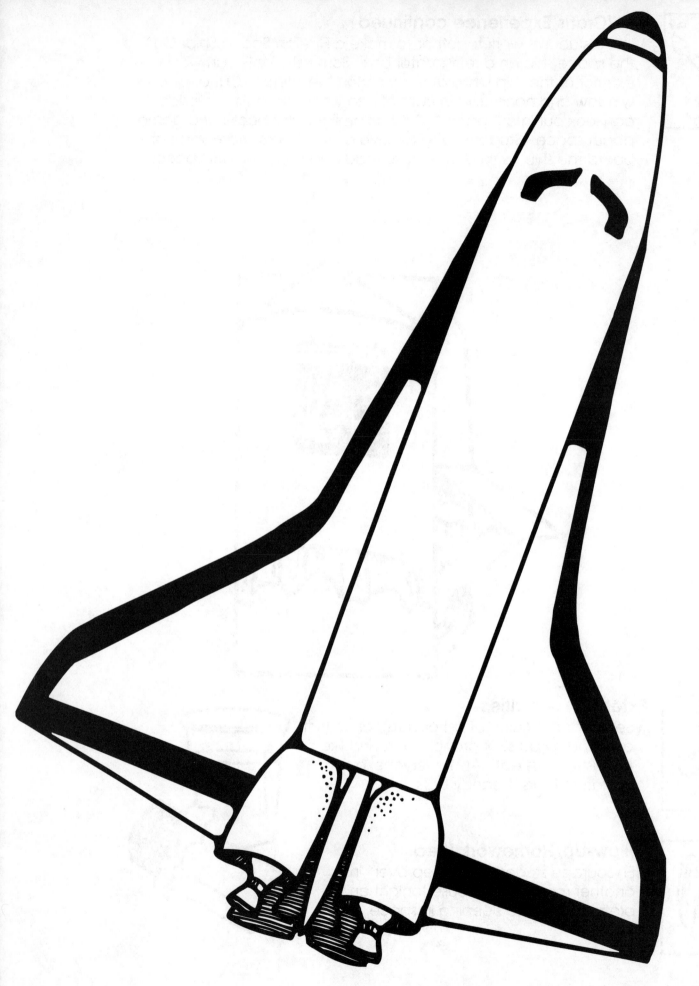

144

I love space! ☆ I

Telephone Book Day

February 21

Setting the Stage

• Beg, borrow and plead for all the telephone books you can get your hands on! Display them around a real or play telephone.

Historical Background

On this day in 1878, the first telephone directory was published in New Haven, Connecticut. It was one page long with 50 names.

146

Language Experience

• Divide your class into groups of two or three (depending on how many phone books you have). Let students search phone books for compound words, 10 short vowel words or whatever you are currently studying.

• Make a class phone book with student names, addresses and phone numbers. Have students alphabetize the names as in a real telephone book.

Writing Experience

• Let students imagine they have their own businesses and write advertisements for them for the yellow pages.

• Have students write about the most interesting name or business in the phone book. (Give them some time to look through a phone book first.)

Math Experience

• Have students measure the area, perimeter and weight of different phone books.

• Older students might want to estimate the number of listings in a phone book. Then they can see how close they are by counting the listings on one page and multiplying that number by the number of pages in the book.

Science/Health Experience

• Have students compile listings of health-related services in the phone book yellow pages.

Music/Dramatic Experience

• Let students look up specific jobs in the yellow pages, then pantomime the jobs for other students to guess.

• Challenge students to read aloud portions of the phone book with great drama as if reading an exciting novel.

Physical/Sensory Experience

• How about a scavenger hunt through the phone book? Make a list of things to search for: a plumber, a woman named Edna, an address with 31 in it, the name of a government agency or an interesting name on page 82. Let students complete as many of these as possible before you call "times up."

Arts/Crafts Experience

• Point out that the phone company might be tired of the old cover of the phone book, and may be looking for a new design. Let students create new cover designs to be submitted for approval.

Follow-Up/Homework Idea

• Encourage students to look up important phone numbers in their phone books (doctor, dentist, veterinarian, etc.) and mark them for easy reference.

George Washington's Birthday

February 22

Setting the Stage

• Display pictures and books about George Washington.

• Construct a semantic web with facts your students already know about George Washington. Ask them to list questions they would like answered.

Historical Background

Today marks the birthday of "The Father of Our Country," George Washington. He was born on this day in 1732.

Literary Exploration

George and the Cherry Tree by Aliki
George Washington by Ingri d'Aulaire, et al
George Washington by Clara Ingram Judson
George Washington by Tom McGowen
George Washington by Kathie Smith
George Washington by Vivian Thompson
George Washington: First President of the United States by Carol Greene
George Washington: A Picture Book Biography by James Cross Giblin
George Washington's Breakfast by Jean Fritz
George Washington's Cows by David Small
George Washington's World by Genevieve Foster
Hello, George Washington! by Janice Holland

Literary Exploration continued

I Did It with My Hatchet: A Story of George Washington by Robert
   Quackenbush
The Joke's on George by Michael O. Tunnell
Meet George Washington by Joan Heilbroner
A Picture Book of George Washington by David A. Adler, et al
The Story of George Washington by May McNeer
The Story of George Washington: Quiet Hero by Joyce Milton
The Story of Mount Vernon by Natalie Miller
Young George Washington: America's First President by Andrew Woods

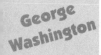

Language Experience

- Create a Venn diagram depicting the similarities and differences between George Washington and Abraham Lincoln.

Writing Experience

- Abraham Lincoln once said that the man who influenced his life was George Washington. Give students opportunity to write about who has made a great influence on their lives. See reproducible on page 154.

Who has had an **influence** on my life?

150

Social Studies Experience

• Share biographical information about George Washington and his presidency.

• Let interested students research Washington's leadership of the Continental Army during the Revolutionary War and share their findings with the class.

Music/Dramatic Experience

• Sing or play recordings of patriotic music.

• After making tri-cornered Washington hats, (see page 152) sing "My Hat, It Has Three Corners."

Physical/Sensory Experience

• Play The Minutemen game. One student is designated the "Minuteman" and the rest are British soldiers. The Minuteman faces away from the British soldiers while they creep up on him or her. When you say, "The British are coming!" the Minuteman turns around and tries to tag as many of the soldiers as possible. Those tagged become Minutemen.

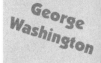

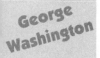

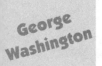

Arts/Crafts Experience

- Give each student a white paper plate on which to draw a portrait of young George Washington wearing a blue patriot hat with gold glitter on the edges. They can add a gray wig and a blue and white collar with a big, gold glitter button at his throat. The details are what count in this portrait of a patriot.

- Give each student a shield shape. They paint the shield to resemble the American flag. While it is drying, students draw self-portraits. They cut them out and glue them onto the shield with the caption: "What's more American than I am?"

- Students can make George Washington Patriot Hats by cutting three 12" x 4" hat shapes from black construction paper. They staple them together at the corners, each to fit his or her head.

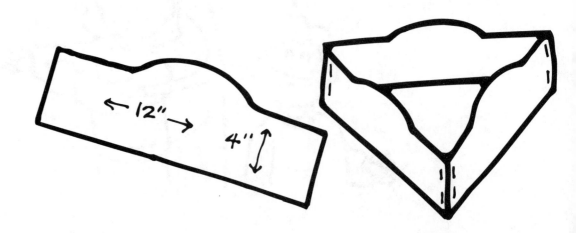

152

TLC10467 Copyright © Teaching & Learning Company, Carthage, IL 62321-0010

Extension Activities

 Tell the legend of young George chopping down a cherry tree, then serve fresh or canned cherries, or make delicious cherry tarts. Give each student a biscuit from refrigerator biscuit dough. They flatten out their biscuits, then spoon canned cherry filling on the inside of one half. They fold over the other side of the biscuit and press the edges together. The edges can be pressed with a fork like a pie crust. Bake according to the refrigerator dough directions. You'll have a yummy treat!

George Washington

Values Education Experience

• George Washington was known for his unselfishness and concern for others. He served as commander of the American forces during the Revolutionary War without any pay. He subjected himself to the same poor circumstances as his men because he didn't think he should be well fed and warm if his men were not. Discuss the kind of leader Washington was and how his leadership inspired those who might otherwise have quit a fight that sometimes looked like a losing cause.

George Washington

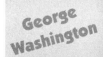

George Washington

Who has had an influence on my life?

George Frederick Handel's Birthday

February 23

Setting the Stage

• Display classical music posters, tapes and CDs.

• Construct a semantic web with facts your students know (or would like to know) about classical music.

Historical Background

The German-English composer, George Frederick Handel, was born on this day in 1685. Some sources give his birthday as February 24, but the 23rd is the generally accepted date.

Language Experience

• How many new words can your students make using the letters in *George Frederick Handel*?

Writing Experience

- Handel was considered a child prodigy. Explain what that means. Then ask students to imagine they are child prodigys. Have them write about what they are extremely gifted in and what they think their lives will be like. See reproducible on page 159.

My Gifts

Social Studies Experience

- Learn about the life of Handel, the great musician and composer.

- Challenge students to do some history research to discover what else was happening in the world while Handel was writing music from about 1700 to 1750.

Music/Dramatic Experience

- Play some of Handel's music ("Hallelujah Chorus" or "Music for the Royal Fireworks") for your class to listen to.

George Frederick Handel

George Frederick Handel

George Frederick Handel

Physical/Sensory Experience

- Play musical chairs to some of Handel's music.

- Play some of Handel's music and let students pretend to direct the orchestra or play the instruments.

Arts/Crafts Experience

- Let students paint with Handel's music to inspire them.

Extension Activities

⚠ Handel was trained in German music, mastered the Italian opera but lived in England. Serve German and Italian sausage on English Muffins. Or bring "Symphony™" candy bars for everyone!

- Invite a composer to your class to talk about his or her work.

George Frederick Handel

George Frederick Handel

George Frederick Handel

Values Education Experience
• Talk about the importance of using our gifts and talents wisely to benefit others.

Follow-Up/Homework Idea
• Encourage students to listen to classical music with their families on the radio, TV or on CD.

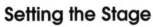

Winslow Homer's Birthday

February 24

Setting the Stage
• Display some prints of Winslow Homer's artwork.

Historical Background
The American artist, Winslow Homer, was born on this day in 1836.

Literary Exploration

Winslow Homer: America's Old Master by Linda Hyman
Winslow Homer the Gulf Stream by Ernest Goldstein, et al

Writing Experience

• Have students look at some of Winslow Homer's paintings, then have each choose one to write about. They should explain what they think is happening in the pictures, making stories about them.

Winslow Homer

Social Studies Experience

• Learn about the life of Winslow Homer. Your students may not be aware that Homer originally sketched soldiers during the Civil War before devoting his life to painting.

Physical/Sensory Experience

• One of Homer's paintings is titled *Snap the Whip* which is a favorite old children's game. Play the game of Snap the Whip with your class. Students join hands in a long line and run. The first person in line stops suddenly, yanking the rest of the line sideways to "snap the whip." Since this can be too rough for some students, you may prefer to just have a few older ones demonstrate it.

Winslow Homer

Arts/Crafts Experience

• Study and critique Homer's art style, then let students paint their own versions of Homer's paintings.

Winslow Homer

Winslow Homer

Extension Activities
- Invite a painter to come and talk about his or her work.

- Visit a nearby art gallery or museum. Encourage students to observe the paintings and try to understand them.

⚠ Make Paintbrush Cookies. Purchase refrigerator sugar cookie dough. Let students "paint" cookies with a mixture of sugar and food coloring (add water to icing for the right consistency). Bake according to the package instructions, then let students eat their artwork.

Follow-Up/Homework Idea
- Challenge students to paint a new picture of something at home then bring it to class to share.

Taxes Day

February 25

Setting the Stage

- Display income tax forms and sales receipts that show tax charges. Explain that today you will be talking about how taxes are paid by people and companies to the government to help pay for services needed to run the country. Students may not be aware that schools, public libraries, parks and the roads as well as salaries for teachers, police officers and government officials are all paid by taxes.

- Construct a semantic map with facts students know (or want to know) about taxes.

Historical Background

Oregon became the first state to tax gasoline on this day in 1919. Now gasoline and most other items are taxed in most states.

Literary Exploration

Taxation: Paying for Government by Charles Hirsch
Taxes by Barbara Sapinsley

Writing Experience

- Ask students to write their feelings about taxes. They should think what our country might be like if people did not support the government through taxation. See reproducible on page 166.

If we didn't have TAXES

Taxes

Math Experience

- Teach students about "real-life" economics by illustrating the taxes taken out of a paycheck. Figure what percentage of taxes goes to education as well as what goes to labor, defense, commerce, welfare, research, conservation and Social Security.

Taxes

Social Studies Experience

- Discuss the history of taxation and its purposes. Talk about why people have rebelled at unfair taxes (such as in the early days of this country just prior to the Revolutionary War). Study the reason for the protest "Taxation without Representation!"

Taxes

Music/Dramatic Experience

• Share the story of early colonists and the Boston Tea Party when they refused to pay taxes to the King of England. Have students role-play that event.

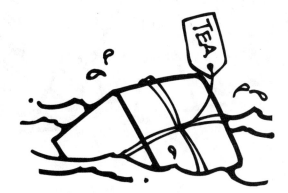

Extension Activities

• Invite a tax preparation specialist to come and explain his or her work to the class.

Follow-Up/Homework Idea

• Encourage students to talk about taxes with their parents.

If we didn't have **TAXES**...

Levi Strauss' Birthday

February 26

Levi
Strauss

Levi
Strauss

Levi
Strauss

Setting the Stage

• Display different sizes, shapes and colors of jeans! Invite students to wear blue jeans today!

• Display a pair of blue jeans on a bulletin board. Attach additional handmade "pockets." Place learning center activities in the pockets. Use the caption: "A Pocketful of Learning Fun!"

• Construct a semantic web with facts your students already know (or want to know) about blue jeans.

Historical Background

Levi Strauss, inventor of blue jeans, was born on this day in 1829. Strauss was born in Bavaria and migrated to America with a dream of making it big. He sold heavy canvas tents, but the demand was not what he thought it would be. Someone suggested he make pants out of the same material. Gold miners in California at that time needed sturdy, durable pants. Strauss added copper rivets to the pant pockets so they wouldn't tear. He called his pants "Levis."

Literary Exploration

Everyone Knows His Name: A Biography of Levi Strauss by Sondra Henry and Emily Taitz

Levi Strauss: Blue Jean Tycoon by Meish Goldish

Levi Strauss: The Blue Jeans Man by Elzabeth Van Steenwyk

Mr. Blue Jeans: A Story About Levi Strauss by MaryAnn Weidt

Science/Health Experience

- Perform scientific tests on blue jeans to test for strength and resiliency (fold or crumple them, pull on them, stomp on them, spill something on them, etc.). Be sure to use an old pair!

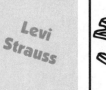

Social Studies Experience

- Learn about the history of blue jeans. Have students research the popularity of blue jeans around the world today.

Music/Dramatic Experience

- Let your students advertise a new kind of blue jeans or create commercials for their old denim favorites.

- Play jazz music and let students sing "the blues" about their jeans.

Extension Activities

⚠ Serve "pocket" pita bread sandwiches.

Poem in My Pocket Day

February 27

Setting the Stage

• Display a large paper tree with full branches on a bulletin board. Put student poetry on leaf shapes and hang them on the branches. Add the caption: "Our POET-Tree"! See leaf pattern on page 174.

• Henry Wadsworth Longfellow was the first American poet to have a memorial in his honor in the Poets' Corner at Westminster Abbey in London. Set aside a Poet's Corner with poetry books, poems on chart paper, writing paper and writing tools so students can go there to write or read poetry.

Fishy fishy in the brook, Daddy caught him with a hook, Momma fried him in a pan, Baby ate him like a man!

I eat my peas with honey, I've done it all my life; It makes my peas taste funny, But it keeps 'em on my knife!

POETRY CORNER

• Construct a semantic web with words your students think of when they hear the word, *poetry*.

Historical Background

The poet, Henry Wadsworth Longfellow, was born on this day in 1807.

Poem in My Pocket

Literary Exploration

The Golden Books Family Treasury of Poetry by Louis Untermeyer
Hailstones and Halibut Bones by Mary O'Neill
I Know an Old Lady Who Swallowed a Fly by Nadine Bernard Westcott
I'll Be You and You Be Me by Ruth Krauss
A Light in the Attic by Shel Silverstein
Nathaniel Talking by Eloise Greenfield
The New Kid on the Block by Jack Prelutsky
Paul Revere's Ride by Henry Wadsworth Longfellow
Pterodactyls and Pizza by Lee Bennett Hopkins
Random House Book of Poetry for Children by Jack Prelutsky
Read-Aloud Rhymes for the Very Young by Jack Prelutsky
Side by Side: Poems to Read Together by Lee Bennett Hopkins
Sing a Song of Popcorn by Beatrice de Regniers, et al
Something Big Has Been Here by Jack Prelutsky
Song of Hiawatha by Henry Wadsworth Longfellow
Where the Sidewalk Ends by Shel Silverstein

Poem in My Pocket

Language Experience

• This is a perfect day to introduce a poetry unit! Explore the various styles: couplets, triangular triplets, chinquapins, limericks, haikus, diamantes, alliterations, acrostics and free verse.

• Teach students the choral poetry reading, "Keep a Poem in Your Pocket," by Beatrice Schenk de Regniers.

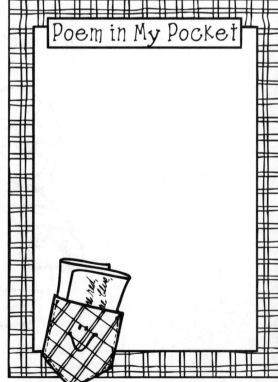

Poem in My Pocket

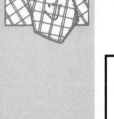

Poem in My Pocket

Writing Experience

• Begin teaching students how to write various styles of poetry.

• Challenge each student to write a short poem of any kind about your school. Post the poems in the hallway for other students to read. See the reproducible on page 173.

Social Studies Experience

• Learn about some of the great poets throughout history. Students can do extra research and share their findings with the class.

Music/Dramatic Experience

• Let students read their favorite poems aloud to a musical background. Encourage them to read with feeling and enthusiasm.

Physical/Sensory Experience

• Let students come up with rhythmic actions to accompany their favorite poetry. These might include finger snapping, hand clapping, foot tapping or stomping, etc.

Extension Activities

• Invite a poet (or someone whose hobby is poetry) to share some of his or her favorite poems with your class.

Values Education Experience

• Discuss what Henry Wadsworth Longfellow meant when he said:
    "All strength is in your union;
    All danger is in discord.
    Therefore be at peace henceforward,
    And as brothers live together."
Ask students to define *union* and *discord*.

Follow-Up/Homework Idea

• Challenge students to write poems about their families. After they share them with their families, they can bring them to class and read them aloud.

Poem in My Pocket

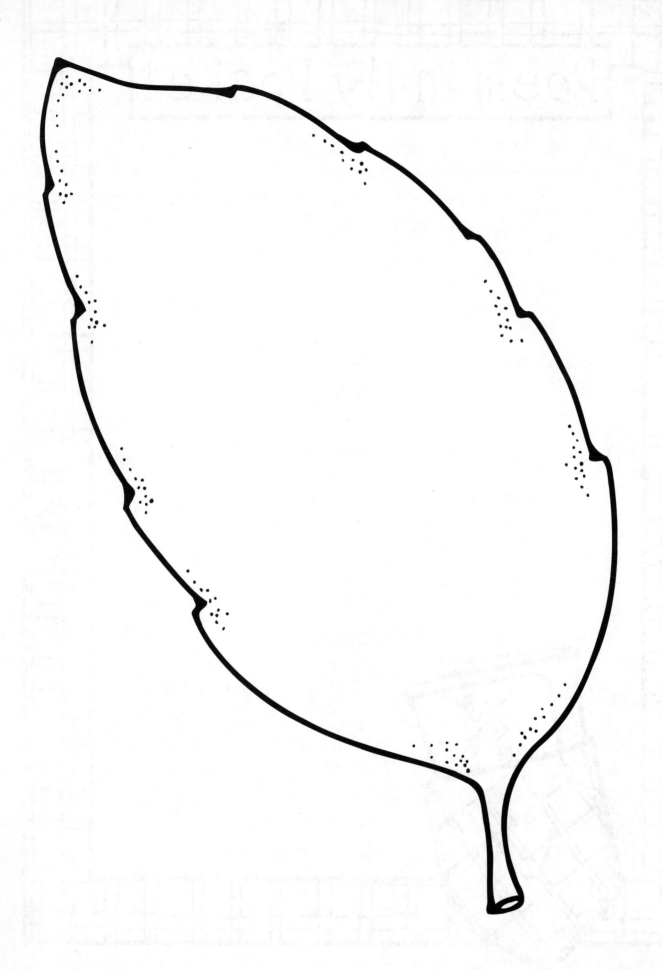

174

Pizza Pizzazz Day

February 28

Setting the Stage

• Have students decorate paper pizza slices with toppings and their names in cheese. Mount them on a bulletin board with the caption: "No matter how you slice it, school is yummy!" See patterns on page 182.

• Ask a local pizza restaurant to donate pizza advertisements or place mats to stimulate and add interest in today's celebration. Some may even donate cardboard boxes or circles upon which the pizzas are placed.

• Construct a semantic map or web with facts the students already know about pizza. Let them list things they want to learn about pizza today.

Historical Background

Pizza has been around since the sixth century b.c. When Persian soldiers baked flat bread on their shields and melted cheese on it for a tasty meal. Pizza came to America in the latter part of the 1800s. The first pizzeria was opened in New York City in 1905. But it didn't become popular until after World War II, when returning soldiers who had eaten pizza in Italy decided they wanted it in America, too. It became one of America's favorite specialty foods.

Literary Exploration

Curious George and the Pizza by Margaret and H.A. Reys

"Hi, Pizza Man!" by Virginia Walter

How Pizza Came to Queens by Dayal Kaur Khalsa

Magic Pizza by Beverly Major Schwartz, et al

The Pizza Book by Stephen Krensky

Pizza for Breakfast by Maryann Kovalski

Pizza Man by Marjorie Pillar

Pizza Soup by Fay Robinson

Pterodactyls and Pizza by Lee Bennett Hopkins

Language Experience

• Reinforce sequencing skills with this activity. Write the following instructions on individual paper strips:

> Wash hands.
> Prepare dough.
> Spread pizza sauce.
> Sprinkle cheese on top.
> Put on pepperoni slices.
> Bake in oven.
> Wash hands and clean up.
> Eat and enjoy!

Mix up the order of the sentence strips and have students arrange them in sequential order. They can work individually or in small groups. Give them paper divided into eight pizza sections with lines (eight sections in all). Let them write the instructions, one on each section. See pattern on page 183.

Pizza
Pizzazz

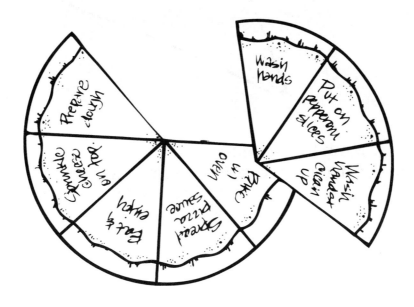

Pizza
Pizzazz

• Let students decorate another copy of page 183 like a real pizza with their favorite toppings. They can staple the pizzas together, then lift up the top one to reveal the instructions underneath.

• Brainstorm various pizza toppings together, then let students alphabetize them!

Pizza
Pizzazz

Writing Experience

• Let students create their favorite pizza recipes! Have them list favorite toppings to the recipe and tell how to assemble the pizza and bake it. Let them write the recipe on the pattern on page 184.

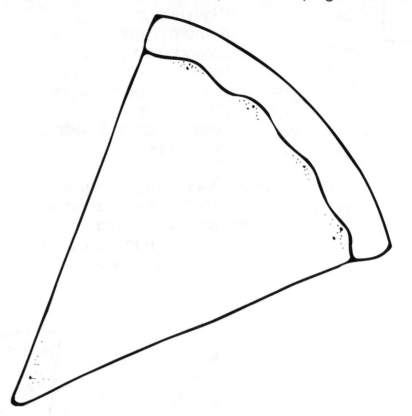

Math Experience

• Students can create "math"-watering skills practice with this fun activity! Provide a pizza shape divided into eight sections. Have students put a number in each section. Give them manipulatives and let them come up with math combinations to fit the numbers. (Example: A pie section with a 6 on it could be used for math problems such as 10 - 4, 3 + 3, 14 - 8 or 3 x 2.)

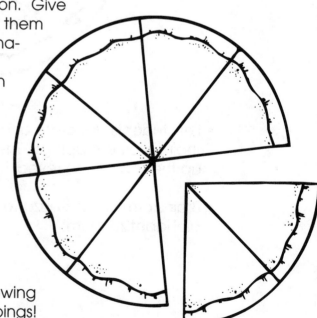

• Review or begin a unit on fractions with different pizza section combinations ($1/4$, $1/2$ or $3/4$). See pattern on page 183.

• Make a class bar graph showing students' favorite pizza toppings!

Social Studies Experience

- Research the beginning of pizza. Where did it come from? Where did it become popular?

Music/Dramatic Experience

- Let students attempt to debate the issue of whether or not pizza can be considered a healthy meal or not (depending on how it's made and its toppings).

Physical/Sensory Experience

⚠ Challenge students to eat pizza without using their hands!

⚠ Let students demonstrate different ways to eat pizza (topping first, folded over, rolled up, upside down, etc.).

- Blindfold students one at a time and play Pin the Topping on the Pizza (a variation of Pin the Tail on the Donkey).

Pizza Pizzazz

Pizza Pizzazz

Pizza Pizzazz

Arts/Crafts Experience

• Have students make tissue collages by glueing tiny squares of colored tissue paper on pizza shapes. Use colors such as orange or yellow for cheese and red for sauce and pepperoni. Show students how to put a small tissue paper square on the end of a pencil eraser, dip it into a dab of glue and put it on a section of pie. Make the pie look full and three-dimensional. Looks good enough to eat!

Extension Activities

• Take students on a field trip to visit a pizzeria to see how they make pizza.

⚠ Miniature pizzas can be made from frozen bread dough, refrigerator biscuits or English muffin halves for crust. Add additional ingredients such as tomato sauce, grated cheese, olives and pepperoni or mushrooms. For an even quicker snack, put pizza sauce with shredded cheese on a round cracker!

⚠ Check at your local grocery store for "peel-able" fruit snacks in pizza shapes.

180

Extension Activities continued

• Let students make pizza faces! After spreading the pizza sauce, let them be creative, making facial features with toppings.

Values Education Experience

• Discuss how each of us makes up "part" of a group that contributes to a greater "whole." Discuss teamwork and how each unique personality adds to the "flavor" of the whole group.

Follow-Up/Homework Idea

• Students can ask their parents to order or make pizza tonight!

Pizza
Pizzazz

Pizza
Pizzazz

Pizza
Pizzazz

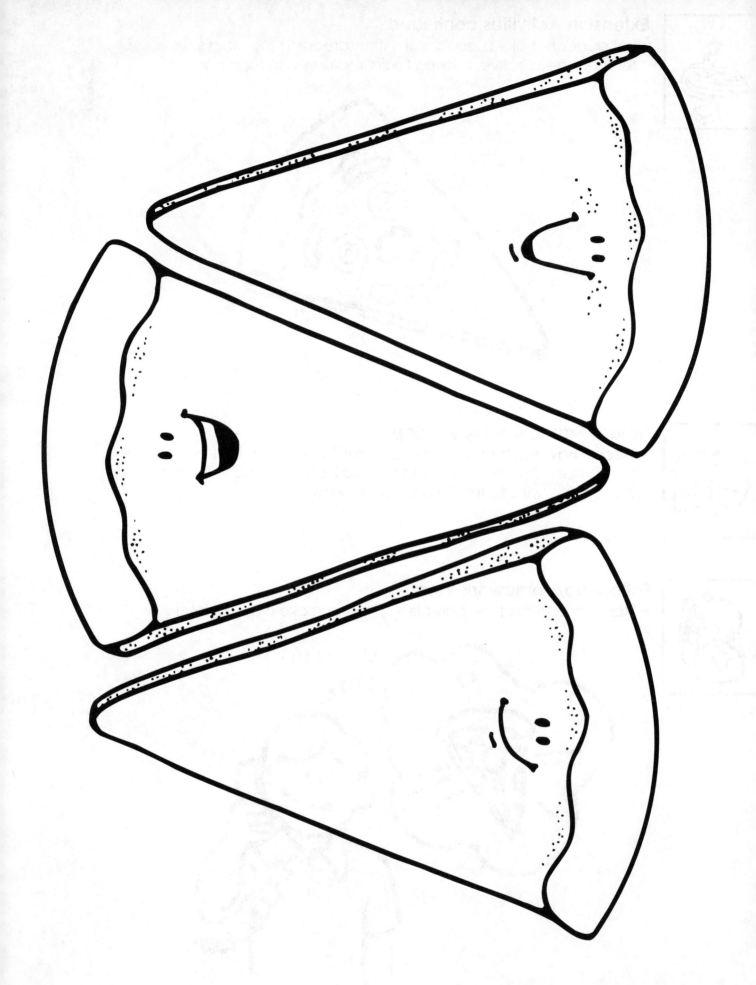

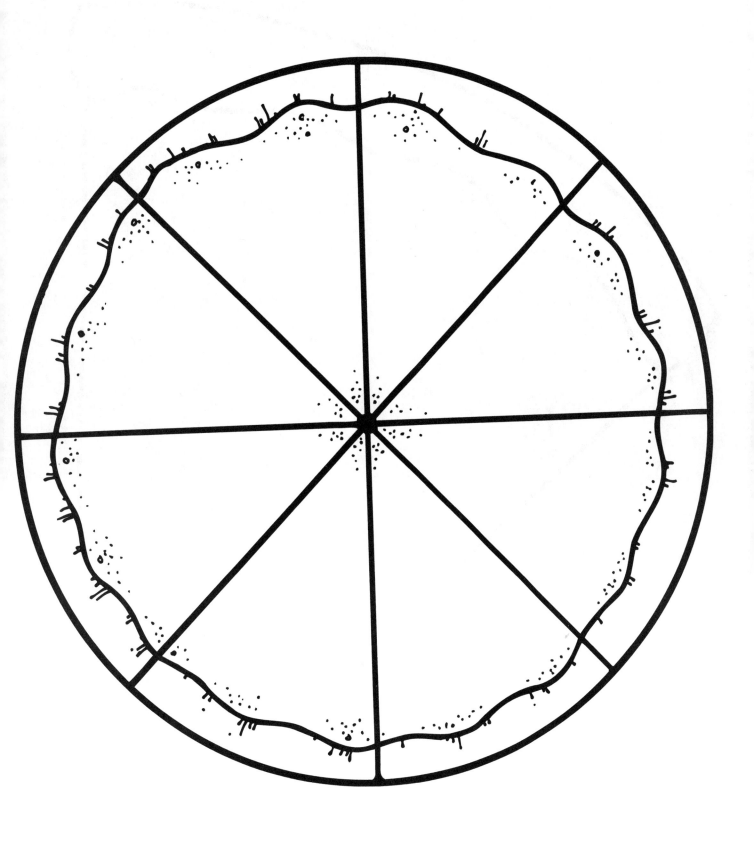

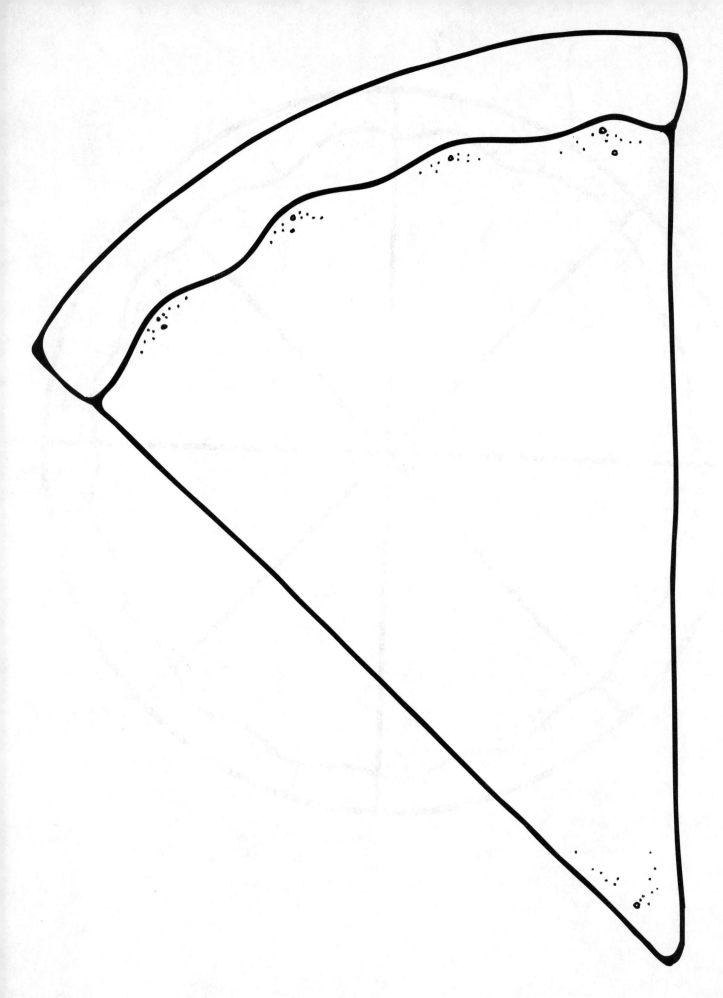

184

Leap Year Day

February 29

Setting the Stage

• Display a large frog on a bulletin board with the caption: "This year we're learning by LEAPS and bounds!" See reproducible on page 188.

Historical Background

Every four years, a year has 366 days rather than 365. That extra day occurs in February—today, February 29th.

Literary Exploration

Fenton's Leap by Libba Moore Gray
One Giant Leap by Mary Ann Fraser
Polar Bear Leaps by Derek Hall
The Sheep Made a Leap by Hilda Offen

Language Experience

• Let your students brainstorm words that rhyme with *leap*.

Writing Experience

- Ask your students to write about what they would like to "skip" or "leap" over. See reproducible on page 189.

Math Experience

- Challenge students to figure out how old they would be if they had been born on February 29th.

- Today is a great day to work on skip (or leap) counting! Teach or review counting by 2s, 5s, 10s or 100s.

Science/Health Experience

- Learn about frogs and their habitat.

- See how many other creatures students can name that hop or leap instead of walking or running.

186

Social Studies Experience

• Have students research Leap Year Day customs around the world. (Example: In Scotland there is an old law that a woman can ask a man to marry her on this day and if the man refuses, he has to pay her 100 pounds in cash. Other countries similarly adopted the same custom, though it is no longer enforced in any country.)

Physical/Sensory Experience

• Play a game of leapfrog!

• Play some lively music and let students skip or leap to it.

Arts/Crafts Experience

• Paint or color frogs leaping across the page. Use pattern on page 190.

Follow-Up/Homework Idea

• Challenge students to "leap" into bed without having to be asked at bedtime tonight.

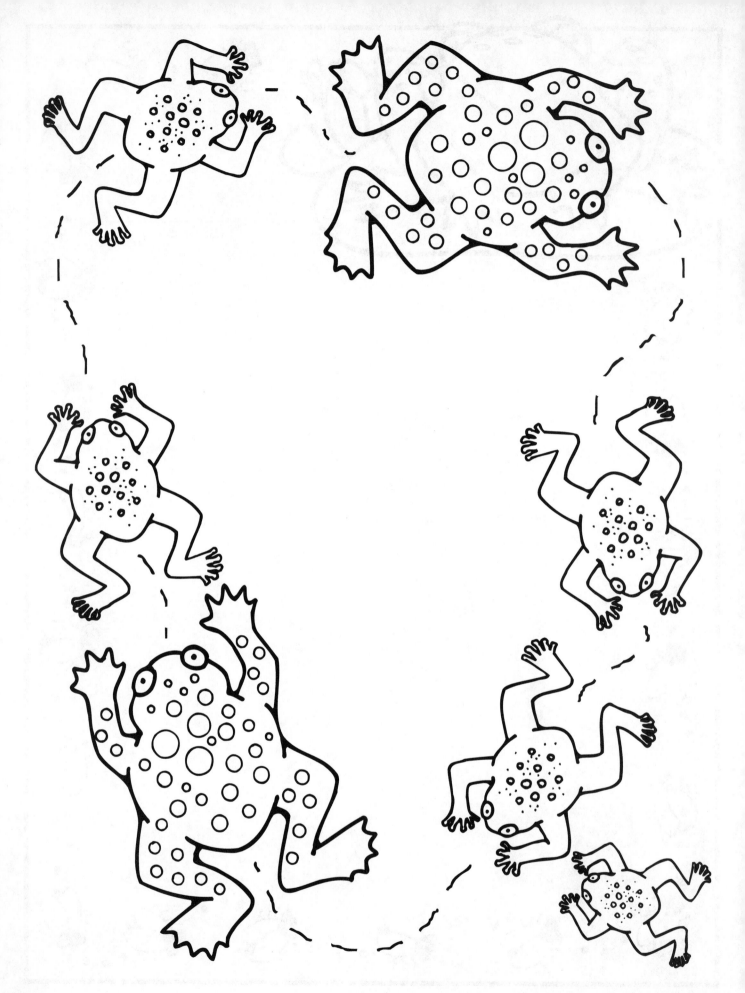

190

February

February

February

February

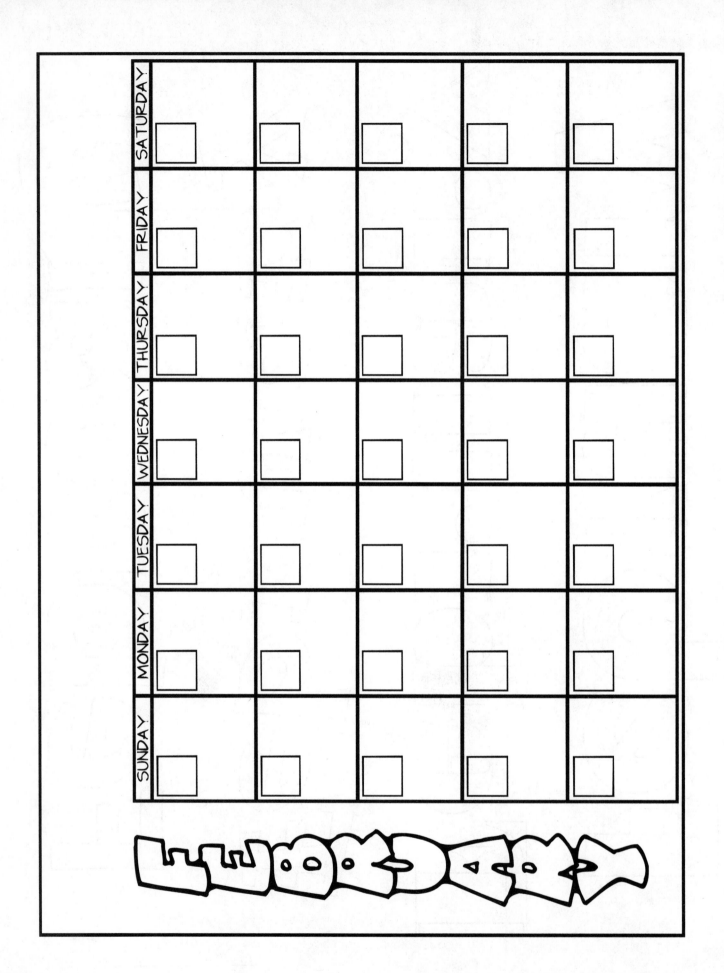